Cinema
&
Society

Cinema & Society

FRANCE AND GERMANY DURING THE TWENTIES

PAUL MONACO

NORTHWEST COMMUNITY COLLEGE

ELSEVIER

New York/Oxford/Amsterdam

ELSEVIER SCIENTIFIC PUBLISHING COMPANY, INC.
52 Vanderbilt Avenue, New York, N.Y. 10017

ELSEVIER SCIENTIFIC PUBLISHING COMPANY
335 Jan Van Galenstraat, P.O. Box 211
Amsterdam, The Netherlands

Library of Congress Cataloging in Publication Data

Monaco, Paul.
  Cinema and society.

  Based on the author's thesis, Brandeis University, 1973,
presented under title: Cinema and society in France and
Germany, 1919–29.
  Bibliography: p.
  Includes index.
    1. Moving-pictures—Social aspects. 2. Moving-pictures—
France—History. 3. Moving-pictures—Germany—History.
I. Title.
PN1995.9.S6M6   791.43'013   75-40650
ISBN 0-444-99019-4

Manufactured in the United States of America

Designed by Loretta Li

Contents

Acknowledgments

The research for this book was completed in France and Germany with the financial support of the Sachar Fellowship Fund of Brandeis University and the German Academic Exchange Service (DAAD). Several libraries and archives were the main sources for the book's documentation. The staffs of all of these institutions were helpful to the author: in France, the Library of Idhec, the Bibliothèque Nationale and its annex in Versailles; in Germany, the Deutsche Kinemathek (Berlin), the Deutsches Institut für Filmkunde (Biberich), the Federal Archives (Koblenz), the Film and Television Academy (Munich), and the Landesbildstelle (Berlin). It was especially important to the success of this project to be able to view as many of the films that are written about in this book as possible. The logistics of movie research are particularly demanding. I am very appreciative of Herr Schulz of the Deutsche Kinemathek, Herr Lichtenstein of the State Film Archives of the German Democratic Republic, and Madame Meerson of the

Cinémathéque française for the cooperation they extended to me in this regard. The Cinémathèque Royale de Belgique also arranged for me to see several films of the 1920s that were not available elsewhere.

Interviews did not form a major part of the research. Nonetheless, I thank Dr. Klaus Kreimeier, Lotte Eisner, and the late Henri Diamant-Berger for the time they afforded to me for discussion of the topic. Eberhard Spiess of the Deutsches Institut für Filmkunde guided me to several sources to which otherwise I might have given less attention. Franz-Josef Albersmeier of Regensburg University read most of the first draft before its completion, and Karin Hausen of the Free University (West Berlin) and William Kirby of Harvard University read parts of it. My mother, Birdena Monaco, typed the final manuscript. My greatest thanks go to Professor Rudolph Binion of Brandeis University. For some three years he prodded, challenged, and guided me in my research. I cannot adequately express to him my appreciation for his help, encouragement, and friendship.

A somewhat different version of Chapter Four of this book first appeared in print as an article in The History of Childhood Quarterly (May 1974). It appears here with the permission of that journal's editor, Lloyd de Mause. The original doctoral dissertation on which this book is based was defended before the Faculty in Comparative History of Brandeis University in September 1973. Its title was Cinema and Society in France and Germany, 1919–29. That original manuscript includes material on the film dream kinship, the relationship of movies to society, and the function of the movie industry in both countries respectively, which is omitted here. There are complete synopses of all 110 most popular films to be found in the original. The author considers this book a complete representation of his research. Some scholars, however, may still wish to refer to the original dissertation after reading this.

All translations from both the French and the German are my own, unless otherwise indicated.

RICHARDSON, TEXAS
DECEMBER 1975

Introduction

Most histories of the cinema emphasize aesthetics. They treat primarily landmark films and innovative techniques, directorial triumphs, and those few films whose contents can be taken seriously enough to be called "art." This study departs from that tradition. It aims to analyze the social function of the cinema in a particular historical setting. Its goal is to interpret comparatively the mass, public meaning of the most popular French and German films of the decade following World War I.

The formulation "film as art" is of limited value historically. To paraphrase the French film historian Charles Ford, those who argue on behalf of the film becoming a more elevated form are right in so doing, but those who accept the cinema for the business that it is are right twice over.[1] More valuable to a historical or sociological treatment of the cinema is the notion expressed in the title of a book by Peter Bächlin, *Der Film als Ware* (*Film as Merchandise*).[2] Traditionally, the producers of feature films do not worry about the medium and what can be done with it artistically; they concentrate, instead, on keeping ahead of the tastes of mass audiences.[3] In this way, their films become—at least hypothetically—a potential source of information about the shared, collective concerns of the group to which those films appeal.

Film being merchandise has meant that movie production has demanded a powerful industry and elaborate business techniques. This, coupled with an awareness of the emotional power of the filmic image, has led many observers to regard the cinema as capable of influencing viewers. From this derives the notion of film as propaganda, a view that develops along two main lines: first, instances in which a film presents a particular ideological message and, second, the more subtle process whereby a seemingly innocuous movie communicates certain values, stereotypes, and received ideas to its viewers. The difficulty with regarding film as propaganda is in attempting to measure the impact of a given movie on individuals or groups. For all the theories and all the studies in this vein, the results have been strikingly unsatisfactory. As the description of a typical study of the influence of films on criminal behavior in the United States during the 1930s accurately and aptly puts it:

> We have set out to determine the effects of motion pictures upon criminals. We did not get much material and most of it is worthless, but it proves that the motion picture is a factor in causing delinquency. But in any event, if it does not prove that, it does prove that the motion picture did not keep delinquents from becoming delinquents.[4]

What this study did indicate—like almost all the work done in this tradition—is that there is just no demonstrating what effect films have on their viewers. Documented examples of behavior having been influenced or modified directly by a film are rare indeed.[5]

Moreover, the capacity of film-makers to manipulate their audiences has, on the whole, been exaggerated. One indication of this is the repeated economic disasters that have befallen large movie-producing firms that gambled on the wrong films. Another is found in the difficulties experienced by the Nazi regime in Germany and by Soviet authorities in Russia in attempting to politicize the content of films in those two countries. After an abortive attempt during the years 1933 and 1934 to gear German film production to propaganda-riddled features, the Nazi Ministry of Propaganda yielded to market considerations. The German film industry then returned to making films along the lines of those produced before Hitler's coming to power.[6] The problem of trying to fulfill Lenin's proclamation—"for us, of all the arts, the cinema is most important"—in Soviet Russia during the 1920s demonstrates the same point. Even an ideologically oriented, state-run film enterprise discovers that it must to some degree respond to the pre-existing tastes of its potential audience. What eventually came to characterize Soviet feature film production was a compromise between the demands of state authorities, the desires of the technicians who actually made the films, and the tastes of the many viewers who went to see them.[7]

Critics of various political persuasions and moral perspectives have repreatedly overestimated the power of the film to communicate information and influence behavior. There is no proof, for example, that pornographic films alter viewers' sexual activities, or that violence in films provokes viewers to violent acts.[8] On the contrary, it is possible that in many instances such films provide for some viewers a healthy, vicarious release of tensions. Assumptions about the impact of film on society, which have been the basis for most of the adventures in movie censorship, are misguided.[9] This is not to say that a given movie may not have "some kind" of effect on a given viewer. It is to emphasize that there is no predicting what the effect of a particular film will be, and no demonstrating historically that the impact of films on behavior has been significant in any society.

Because film production involves exceptionally high unit costs and is, even under the most favorable of circumstances, a high-risk venture, film-makers can rarely afford to give way to their own notions. They must, instead, give play to what they believe are the shared tastes of the mass audience.[10] As Peter Bächlin claims; "The popularity of a film, indeed the very reason for its existence, arises on the whole from the adaptation of its contents to the dominant thoughts, conceptions, and instinctual wishes of contemporary society."[11]

The main source of information on which a film producer bases commercial evaluations of future productions are past films' box-office receipts.[12] This leads to standardization in the cinema of a particular society at a given time. New films are made containing subjects, themes, and dramatic devices that have, during the period immediately preceding, been successful at the box office. The real art of the cinema historically is the artistry of the entrepreneur. To do business is to succeed in appealing to the mass audience through a medium that, according to the economist Jacques Durand, is "more dependent on public taste or changes in style" than any other.[13] This suggests that basic to the social function of the cinema is the extent to which the appeal of movies is collective and, most probably, unconscious. "The secret of success of the best film directors lies in their ability, in one way or another, to produce collective images by creating certain human types, objects, and situations which, thanks to the process of identification, facilitate the public's acceptance of a film."[14]

The difficulty is to move from this understanding to a method for analyzing film as a reflection of the group process in society. The art historian Walter Abell has pointed out a possible approach by writing: ". . . art is one of the cultural symbols into which society projects its existent states of underlying tension. . . . Thus, we are led to conceive of higher forms of cultural expression in any society as manifestations of a 'collective dream.' "[15] In support of his theory, Abell presents examples drawn mainly from literature and architecture. The popular cinema, however, likely offers a better reflection of the shared, collective, latent tensions in society than the works and artifacts of high culture. A film is almost always "essentially a group production."[16] And for that reason alone a popular movie might be expected to have a closer relationship to the group processes in society than an individual artistic creation. The term "mass culture" has meaning, and that meaning is accentuated in the popular cinema. By the end of World War I the movies had established themselves nearly everywhere as the first truly "popular" entertainment of the twentieth century. "The cinemas were cheaper than the previous places of entertainment. They were more comfortable, they were open for longer hours. And they were everywhere—in every town and in many villages. They were also for everybody, without distinction to age, class, or sex."[17]

The product that drew the masses to the movie theaters in the 1920s was the "feature film," usually an hour to two hours in length, dramatic in nature, and often based on an adaptation from a novel or a play. The movie theaters themselves soon came to reflect the mass popularity of the medium. This was the grand era of the palatial movie house, often seating from two to five thousand spectators, decorated in imitation classical or oriental motifs, serviced by ushers and usherettes, and offering full orchestras for musical accompaniment to the silent films. Movie-going had become respectable, which it was not before World War I, as well as popular. After 1918 the audience for movies came quickly to include "le public élégant, the bourgeois, and the workers."[18] Children and adolescents, rarely seen at legitimate theaters, concerts, ballets, or operas, frequented the cinemas, except that certain films were forbidden to youth by censors—a practice that was common worldwide.[19] And in France and Germany, as well as in other Western and Northern European countries and in North America, women commonly went to movie theaters unescorted by men—a social practice hitherto unknown.[20]

The broad popularity of films after World War I was an indication that the cinema of the 1920s was developing an increasingly collective character. Gone were the prewar days when cheap one-reelers could be turned out to appeal to the lower-class audience that patronized the many small and uncomfortable movie theaters located in the poorer sections of cities.[21] Movies had become respectable and popular, and in their own peculiar way they had to be "timely." The feature films that appealed to the mass, national audiences of the 1920s came and went quickly, striking the fancy of millions. In that period most films had runs of less than six months, and they were shown in small towns and rural areas within weeks of having premiered in a big city.[22] The "timeliness" of a popular film was perplexing, however. For there usually seemed to be no overt explanation of why particular movies succeeded when others did not. Howard Lewis, skeptical of the feasibility of analyzing popular films in their relationship to society, expressed this dilemma in his monograph on film-making in the United States during the 1920s: "Outstandingly successful films have appealed to some public interests, but in many cases these interests did not dominate the public mind at the time these pictures appeared. On the contrary, they were more or less latent."[23]

In spite of his skepticism, Lewis unwittingly makes the very point that opens the possibility of analyzing popular films as a reflection of the shared, collective concerns of the audience to which they appealed. There can be little arguing that feature films only rarely are addressed directly to contemporary social problems. Instead, movies find their relationship to society in oblique symbolism. The most fruitful source of insight into an individual's latent concerns is the dream. One of the most striking characteristics of film is its kinship to the dream.

Among the names proposed for the first film projector (introduced publicly in 1895) was "thaumatrope," from the Greek for dream.[24] And although "cinematrograph" won out in the name race, the notion of parallels between film and dream has persisted. ". . . all those who have written about the cinema, from theoreticians to critics, or, in passing, film makers and film fans, have mentioned, in one way or another, the kinship which exists between the film and the dream."[25]

"All" may be an exaggeration, but the real problem is that most of these numerous references neither lead anywhere nor meaningfully stand alone. In popular parlance "dream" can denote a mere wish ("I'm dreaming of a White Christmas") or a cluster of values ("The American Dream") having little relation to dreaming proper. Much talk of the film/dream kinship is that loose. It need not be, however, for the parallels between watching a film and the dream experience are numerous, direct, and literal.

There is no better place to begin a brief description of the film/dream kinship than by citing a quotation from Sigmund Freud's *Interpretation of Dreams*:

> . . . what characterizes the waking state is the fact that thought takes place in concepts and not in *images*. Now our dreams think essentially in images; and with the approach of sleep it is possible to observe how, in proportion as voluntary activities become more involuntary ideas arise, all of which fall into the class of images . . . Dreams then think primarily in terms of visual images.[26]

[7]

All films (and all the more so the silent films being treated in this study) are essentially visual, composed of sequential pictorial images. On this point the more recent research into sleep and dreaming reinforces the film/dream parallel particularly well. David Foulkes summarizes this research in *The Psychology of Sleep*:

> Approximately fifteen years ago, scientists discovered that dreaming occurs during sleep characterized by a particular patterning of the brain wave and by rapid movements of the eyeball, as if the eye were *watching* the pictorial content of a dream. When awakened from this stage of sleep, which occurs periodically through the night, human subjects are almost always able to recall a vivid, perceptual, *hallucinatory* (at the same time it seemed *real*), and somewhat distorted drama that would unhesitatingly be called a dream.[27]

The eye movements of the dreamer are not random but are "associated with the visual characteristics of [his] dream."[28] The same is true of watching a movie: "The film spectator occupies a fixed seat, but only physically . . . Aesthetically he is in permanent motion as his eye identifies with the lens of the camera, which permanently shifts in distance and direction."[29] It is also known that dream sleep is distinguished by changes in brain wave (electroencephalographic) measurements.[30] Remarkably, experimentation has indicated that the same is true of film viewing. Regardless of the visual imagery or the content of a film sequence, watching it produces modified electroencephalographic readings for any viewer.[31] What occurs during a film projection corresponds closely to the physiology of REM (rapid eye movement) dream sleep, producing a state resembling the hypnotic. This is characterized by the slowing down of the alpha wave rhythm in the brain and a tendency for the waves to measure out in patterns of "saw tooth," up, down regularity.[32]

Besides these modifications in the psychomotor comportment of any film viewer, other facets of the film experience merit attention. In movies, instantaneous cuts from one scene to another are common and pose little difficulty for the spectator. This mode of discontinuous presentation is achieved by editing.[33] The most typical way of telling a film story is parallel editing, the first use of which is attributed to an American film director in the first decade of this century:

The Great Train Robbery (1903) by Edwin S. Porter, one of America's pioneer director-photographers, revealed for the first time the function and the power of the cut in telling a story on the screen. . . . We see the robbers enter the station, bind and gag the telegraph operator, then steal aboard the train all in proper sequence. But after they have held up the train and made their getaway, Porter switches back to the unfortunate operator just as he is discovered by his little daughter at the station. The two lines of action are taking place simultaneously—the robbers escaping, the crime discovered.[34]

By comparison, notable in dream recollections recorded by numerous REM researchers is the subject's use of the descriptive phrase: ". . . and then all of a sudden the scene changed."[35] Just that happens in feature films, with a frequency and abruptness duplicated at no other point in human experience save in dreaming. Freud, too, unintentionally pointed up this parallel. He noted that the patient usually reported in dream recollections: "But then it was as though at the same time it was another place, and such and such a thing happened."[36]

Some may regard dreams as vivid visual dramas that pass through the mind's eye in a matter of seconds. Such brevity would then militate against the film/dream kinship. The bulk of the research concludes, however, that dream sequences are "rarely less than ten minutes long and may last for an hour or more."[37] The presence of language in films may also disturb some, for this seems a way in which silent movies might differ from dreams. What words there are in silent films possess a visual existence as printed titles; they explain or elaborate something that occurs visually in the film. Speech in dreams is minimal, and as Freud writes of words and dreams: ". . . (all) spoken sentences which occur in dreams and specifically described as such are ... often no more than an allusion to some event included (visually) among the dream thoughts."[38]

The dark magic-cave enviroment of the movie theater, the uninterrupted nature of a film showing, the rhythmic luminosity of the projection itself, and the social isolation of the spectator combine to create the near-hypnotic state that characterizes movie viewing. "In dreams, daily life with its labors and pleasures, its joys and pains, is never repeated. On the contrary, dreams have as their very aim to free us from it."[39] Feature films do not simply recreate daily reality any more than a dream does. Both the film viewer and the dreamer experience a kind of hyper-reality: exceptional events portrayed in minute detail. Both films and dreams select out situations and moods close to normal life and express the drama in them with pictorial intensity. Dreamlike, "the art of the cinema is summed up by two opposing tendencies—escape from reality and the accentuation of reality."[40]

Striking parallels all along the line between film and dream indicate that films, like dreams, may have latent meanings. Freud called the dream a "picture puzzle," claiming that his predecessors had made the error of regarding dreams as "pictorial compositions" that seemed to them to be "nonsensical and worthless."[41] In the same manner, popular films have long been regarded as historically worthless and inconsequential when viewed as works of art. Freud recognized that the successful dream work will tend to yield a dream that coheres on the surface ("secondary elaboration" in Freud's terminology). The findings of the REM researchers indicate even more strongly that "dreams generally do have coherent plots."[42] Through elaborate plots and often overemphatic resolutions, films may well disguise their underlying meaning.

Proceeding from the surface film/dream kinship, the object of this study is to analyze the most popular native-produced films of France and Germany as dreamlike reflections of shared, collective concerns of the mass, national audience. A cornerstone of this method is the emphasis placed on *popular* films. Suprisingly, perhaps, the list of most popular films that could be documented for the two countries in the period 1919–29 cuts across standards of quality. It includes several well-known film classics, an array of mediocre movies, and some glaring examples of commercial movie-making at its worst. Here the treatment of these films is not intended to be critical; there is already an ample literature on film as art in both countries during the period. Rather, the assumption is that in a cluster of popular films that cuts across aesthetic considerations there are certain motifs and images common to these films that determine their popularity.

The analytical method by which the popular films of a nation are treated as a dreamlike reflection of the nation's collective psyche parallels the analysis of individual dreams. In the first instance, it seeks to identify the pictorial compositions that *repeat* from one film to the next. And, making adjustments to deal with a collective phenomenon, the methodology follows the Freudian line, which, in general, has been reinforced rather than challenged by the findings of the REM researchers. They have concluded that dreams are, indeed, understandable in light of the "dreamer's contemporary waking life, in particular the conflicts, anxieties, and tensions which have recently assumed a salient position in his waking adjustment," and, also, "the historical roots in the dreamer's earlier experiences of his present difficulties."[43] At the collective level the "dreamer's contemporary waking life" is composed of the concerns and problems born of the group's recent history (the preconscious level). The "historical roots" (unconscious level) are formed from the earlier history of the group insofar as it relates to present dilemmas. If it can be documented that a particular set of popular films was made for, and appealed to, a particular national audience, then the interpretive work can be accomplished because the analyst can come to terms with that nation's history—the very stuff out of which both the conscious and the unconscious life of the nation is formed. This requires first identifying without prejudice the elements in the most popular films. The second step is to interpret the latent meanings of repeated motifs and images by empathizing with the national history and, while doing so, groping to find the inner sense by which all the pieces fit. The method is properly rigorous because testable (i.e., repeatable) by others.

Enrico Fulchignoni claims that "the movie screen compares to a doctor or a center for analysis to which crowds come to indulge in the rite of recognizing their most secret dreams."[44] In preferring certain films to others, a group is stating something about itself. Whether it recognizes this process for what it is, is unlikely and irrelevant. The interpretive method to be used is flexible in accordance with Freud's own principles, being "prepared to find that the same piece of content may conceal a different meaning when it occurs in various people or in various contents."[45]

The era of the silent film is a closed chapter in the history of popular culture. In both France and Germany the last silent features were produced in 1929. The advent of the "talkies" posed new technical, aesthetic, and commercial problems for film industries everywhere. The decade from 1919 to 1929 was the great era of the silent movie as mass entertainment.

In some ways, other national cinemas were more important—either commercially or aesthetically—than the French and German cinemas during the 1920s. But each of these—the American, the Japanese, and the Soviet—poses its own particular difficulties for a study of film and society. The national cultures, political and social institutions, and film-industry structures in each of the three are too complex to be dealt with in the kind of comparative study being undertaken here. France and Germany did have the two most important film industries in Europe, the Russians aside. The Scandinavian cinema achieved a good deal of critical acclaim immediately following World War I but quickly peaked. The Italian industry was left a shambles in the 1920s by a pair of meddlers: first, the poet D'Annunzio and, in turn, the dictator Mussolini. England's movie production during the period was on again, off again, but mostly off as Hollywood films flooded the country to an extent duplicated nowhere on the Continent.

France and Germany were *roughly* comparable in many ways during the era. The Weimar German constitution was, after all, quite similar to the outline of political institutions that existed in France under the Third Republic. During the 1920s both were something less than completely stable republics. Their industrial and general economic development had not been precisely parallel; still, both were major producing nations and potential competitors in many fields. Intellectually, artistically, culturally, and educationally the countries were most alike—this, indeed, in spite of numerous particular differences between them in each of these areas. With the Soviet Union temporarily isolated from the rest of the world, and with England maintaining an aloofness toward the Continent during most of the 1920s, France and Germany were Europe's two great Continental powers. They were the center, between them, of much of the political activity, social debate, and philosophical malaise that characterized the decade. Clearly, they were not the same yet had similar concerns. Comparable as they were, however, they were barely compatible. Their national dilemmas and crises developed from different origins and took on different forms. Often, however, the difficulties could be boiled down descriptively to some common categorical denominator. In the 1920s France and Germany were the recent enemies of the trenches of World War I and the imminent enemies for a repeat performance that was to be called World War II. To be comparable does not imply being necessarily alike. It is because France and Germany were on opposite sides of the *same* fence that it is interesting to look at them together. Ample documentation indicates that the governments and the populace of France and Germany were very much aware of, and concerned with, each other during the decade following the First World War. The same held for the respective film industries of both nations. They were keen to each other's activities. The French film industry had been the world's most productive before 1914. During the 1920s, however, she found herself hardpressed to live up to her past. Grudgingly, France watched as Germany, whose film industry before 1914 had been feeble, emerged in the great era of the silent film as Europe's foremost producer of movies.

N O T E S

1. Charles Ford, *Bréviaire du cinéma* (Paris: 1945), p. 91.
2. Peter Bächlin, *Der Film als Ware* (Basel: 1947). In similar vein, though presenting a less thorough argument, is Walter Benjamin, *Das Kunstwerk im Zeitalter seiner technischen Reproduzierbarkeit* (Frankfurt a.M.: 1955).
3. Pauline Kael, "Movies: The Desparate Art," in Daniel Talbot, *Film: An Anthology* (Berkeley and Los Angeles: 1967), p. 54.
4. Raymond Moley, *Are We Movie-Made?* (New York: 1938), p. 22, commenting on H. Blumer and P. M. Hauser, *Movies, Delinquency, and Crime* (New York: 1933). Cited also in the annotated bibliography in I. C. Jarvie, *Towards A Sociology of Cinema* (London: 1970).
5. A few spectacular stories, such as the one about a Negro being lynched in Nebraska by movie-goers who were excited by seeing D. W. Griffith's *Birth of A Nation*, circulate without much substantiation. Coincidences of crimes that resemble something depicted in the movies can be counted on to periodically set off speculation on cinema's evil effects. Strict demonstration of cause and effect relationships between films and behavior are, however, unknown to the author.
6. David Stewart Hull, *Film in the Third Reich* (Berkeley and Los Angeles: 1969). Goebbels was forewarned of the limitations and difficulties of politicizing feature films; see Hans Traub, *Der Film als politisches Machtmittel* (Munich: 1933).
7. John Rimberg, *Motion Picture in the Soviet Union, 1918–1952: A Sociological Analysis*, unpublished dissertation, Columbia University, New York, 1959.

8. A sampling of literature of this type suffices to demonstrate the unsatisfactory and inadequate results in trying to measure the "effects" of the film. Many titles could be cited. A few typical ones are: R. S. Albert, "The Role of Mass Media and the Effect of Aggressive Film Content Upon Children," *Psychology Monographs*, 55, 211–85, 1957; Otto N. Larsen, "Social Effects of Mass Communication," in R. E. L. Faris, *Handbook of Modern Sociology* (Chicago: 1964); D. Treacy, *The Effects of Mass Communication: A Survey and Critique*, unpublished dissertation, University of Illinois, Champaign/Urbana, 1966; W. D. Wall, "The Emotional Responses of Adolescent Groups to Certain Films," *British Journal of Educational Psychology*, 21, 81–88, 1959.

9. For example, Mark Koenigal, *Movies in Society* (New York: 1962).

10. Jean Mitry, *Esthétique et psychologie du cinéma* (Paris: 1963), I, p. 33. Also, André Lang, *Déplacements et villégiatures litteraires* (Paris: no date), p. 225.

11. Bächlin, *op. cit.*, p. 15.

12. I. C. Jarvie, *Towards A Sociology of Cinema* (London: 1970), p. 105.

13. Jacques Durand, "Le Film est-il une marchandise?" *Le Cinéma, fait social*, XXVIIème semaine sociale universitaire, 20–25 April 1959, Brussels, p. 40.

14. M. Ponzo, "Le Cinéma et les images collectives," *Revue Internationale de Filmologie*, Tome II, no. 6, 1948, p. 149.

15. Walter Abell, *The Collective Dream in Art* (New York: 1966), p. 5.

16. Margaret Mead, "Why Do We Go to the Movies?" *Redbook Magazine*, March 1971, p. 48. See also Fritz Lang, "Arbeitsgemeinschaft im Film," *Der Kinematograph*, 18. Jahrg., no. 887, 17 February 1924, p. 7, and Eduard Jawitz, "Mein ideales Maunuskript," *Der Film-Kurier*, 6. Jahrg., no. 77, 29 March 1924, p. 3.

17. A. J. P. Taylor, *From Sarajevo to Potsdam* (New York: 1966), p. 97.

18. Georges Sadoul, *Le Cinéma devient un art* (Paris: 1956), p. 442.

19. Claude Bonnefoy, *Le Cinéma et ses mythes* (Paris: 1965), p. 63. Also, Rudolf Oertel, *Filmspiegel* (Vienna: 1941), p. 120.

20. Numerous references. One of the most interesting contemporary commentaries on the movie-going habits of women during the 1920s is found in the Parisian daily *L'Ami du peuple* (Paris), 15 May 1928, p. 8.

21. See Jacques Deslandes and Jacques Richard, *Histoire comparée du cinéma* (Paris: 1968), II. Also, René Jeanne, *Cinéma 1900* (Paris: 1965), as well as G.-Michel Coissac, *Histoire du cinématographe* (Paris: 1925), pp. 346 ff. and Heinrich Fraenkel, *Unsterblicher Film* (Munich: 1956), I, pp. 44 ff. More impressions and histories of the primitive movie theaters of pre-1914 are to be found in numerous other sources. Of particular interest are the tales of the "wagon cinemas" that traveled from town to town in Germany during the first decade of the century.

22. Henri Fescourt, *et al.*, *Le Cinéma des origines à nos jours* (Paris: 1932), p. 143; *Die Lichtbildbühne*, 15. Jahrg., no. 13, 25 March 1922, p. 22; André Lang, *op. cit.*, p. 148; Paul Leglise, *Histoire de la politique du cinéma français: le cinéma et la IIIème république* (Paris: 1970), p. 55.

Howard Lewis, *The Motion Picutre Industry* (New York: 1933), pp. 107, 108, notes the *timeliness* of films in the 1920s. He comments that producers and distributors evidently believed that this category of consideration applied only to audiences for native-produced films—the notion held no validity in regard to films being distributed in a foreign market.

23. Lewis, *op. cit.*, pp. 107, 108.
24. Andreas Freund, "Marking 75 Years of Movies in France," *The International Herald Tribune* (Paris), 29 December 1970, p. 14.
25. No author, "Ecrits psychanalytiques sur le cinéma," *Travail au Film*, no. 1, January 1970, p. 12.
26. Sigmund Freud, *The Interpretation of Dreams*, trans. and ed. by James Strachey (New York: 1965), p. 82. The author's italics.
27. David Foulkes, *The Psychology of Sleep* (New York: 1966), p. 3. Foulkes' italics.
28. Wilse B. Webb, *Sleep: An Experimental Approach* (New York: 1968), p. 81. See also Herman A. Witkins and Helen B. Lewis, *Experimental Studies of Dreaming* (New York: 1967), pp. 19, 51.
29. Edwin Panofsky, "Style and Medium in the Motion Pictures," in Talbot, *op. cit.*, pp. 18, 19.
30. Foulkes, *op. cit.*, pp. 23, 31. Also, Witkins and Lewis, *op. cit.*, pp. 9, 45–47.
31. Gilbert Cohen-Seat, H. Gastaut, and J. Bert, "Modifications de l'E.E.G. pendant la projection cinématographique," *Revue Internationale de Filmologie*, Tome V, no. 16, 1954, p. 20. Also, Henri Gastaut and Annette Roger, "Effets psychologiques, somatiques, electroencephalographiques des stimulus lumineux intermittents rhytmiques," *Revue Internationale de Filmologie*, Tome II, nos 7 & 8, 1948, pp. 215 ff.
32. Y. Galfriet and J. Segal, "Cinéma et physiologie des sensations," *Revue Internationale de Filmologie*, Tome II, nos. 3 & 4, 1948, pp. 292, 293.
33. Raymond Spottiswoode, *A Grammar of the Film* (Berkeley and Los Angeles: 1965), p. 201.
34. Arthur Knight, *The Liveliest Art* (New York and Toronto: 1957), p. 41.
35. Foulkes, *op. cit.*, p. 64.
36. Freud, *op. cit.*, p. 371.
37. Foulkes, *op. cit.*, p. 52.
38. Freud, *op. cit.*, p. 348.
39. *Ibid.*, p. 41.
40. Carl Vincent, *L'Histoire de l'art cinématographique* (Brussels: no date), 2nd ed., p. X. See also Elie Fauré, "The Art of Cineplastics," in Talbot, *op. cit.*, p. 12.
41. Freud, *op. cit.*, pp. 312, 313.
42. Foulkes, *op. cit.*, p. 78.
43. *Ibid.*, pp. 179, 180.
44. Enrico Fulchignoni, *La Civilisation de l'image* (Paris: 1969), pp. 72, 73.
45. Freud, *op cit.*, p. 137.

Film as Big Business in France and Germany in the 1920s

In May 1919 a reporter for the film trade journal *Le Courrier cinématographique* wrote that throughout France movie theaters had been "filled to overflowing" since the armistice of November 1918.[1] The opening address at a conference on cinema held in Paris in 1944 was laced with reminiscences of the droves of spectators who flocked to the cinemas during the months following World War I.[2] And a well-known social history of France in the 1920s and 1930s points out that among the phenomena that characterized French life immediately after 1919 was that movie houses were "overrun" by customers.[3]

Had the cinemas been packed with customers only for a short time right after World War I, or had this striking popularity of movie-going been limited to countries directly affected by the war, then the throngs of film fans might be written off as escapists from "war weariness."[4]

This was not the case. There is evidence that on the eve of World War I the cinema was on the verge of becoming immensely popular, and that in most of Europe the war delayed this development.[5] The broad appeal of the movies after 1918, with some local variations, was worldwide. Audiences flocked to movie theaters all across Europe, in North America, and in some Asian countries as well.[6] Wherever movies were to be seen, seeing them became popular. And it stayed popular. Movie attendance increased everywhere, year by year, during the 1920s. "From being a low-grade diversion it became middle class entertainment and even stylish to go to the movies."[7]

Right after World War I, in both France and Germany as well as in almost every other nation of Europe, construction of new movie theaters boomed. The new cinemas, especially those built in large and middle-sized cities, emphasized size, elegance, comfort, and opulence. Older movie theaters were spruced up, and the new ones were constructed not just to accommodate the growing audiences but also to endow movie-going with an aura of "respectability." Throughout France after 1918 the seating in cinemas improved, musical accompaniments to silent films were provided by talented pianists and sometimes by full orchestras, and spectators took to eating chocolate-covered ice-creams "à la mode américaine."[8] By the beginning of 1919 one of Europe's few large prewar theaters, the Gaumont Palace located at the Place Clichy in Paris, had been outfitted with 5,000 seats, space for 80 musicians in its orchestra pit, a Greco-Roman décor, lush carpeting, assorted statuary, and a fully equipped bar.[9] In April of the same year a new movie theater, which competed with the Gaumont Palace, opened in Paris on the Boulevard des Italiens. The Marivaux was an architectural and decorative mélange of Ionic columns, Egyptian statues, wall-to-wall carpeting, and assorted appropriate accoutrements.[10] In every year during the 1920s the Gaumont Palace and the

Marivaux each drew over four million customers. Two other Parisian movie houses, the Aubert Palace and the Lutetia, were each attracting over two million viewers per year by 1920. In 1924 ten cinemas in Paris reached the two million mark in attendance. Twenty-three other Parisian movie theaters reported over one million paid admissions each year during the 1920s.[11] In 1921 paid admissions to cinemas accounted for 23 percent of total entrances to all "attractions" in the city. By 1929 the percentage had risen to just over 40.[12] The percentages are all the more impressive because they relate cinema admissions to *all* other public attractions. These included paid admissions not only to legitimate theaters, concerts, and operas, but also to circuses, music halls, cabarets, sporting events, recreational areas, public museums, and historical monuments. In other cities and towns throughout France, the cinema's domination of the "attractions" business was almost total. Bordeaux, with a population of 250,000, had 30 large movie theaters in operation by the end of 1919. Across France there was an even distribution of cinemas to population: a movie house for every 9,000 inhabitants. Representatively, Bourges (45,000 population) had 5 movie theaters; Charente, with 38,221 inhabitants, had 4 cinemas; and Tulle, with a population of barely 17,000, had 2.[13] Not only in Paris, but also in the medium-sized and smaller cities, the demand for film entertainment was so great that movie theaters soon initiated daily showings that ran continuously from 10 a.m. until late in the evening. This practice was maintained throughout the 1920s almost without exception.[14] Early in 1920 French Minister of Finance Louis Klotz justified an increase in national taxes on cinema admissions by pointing out that because of the "vogue to which cinema is playing" nationwide, it, better than any other entertainment, could bear the added burden.[15] That "vogue" did not dissipate during the 1920s. In 1923 cinema receipts in France totaled more than 85 million francs. By

1926 the figure had risen to over 145 million. In 1929 movie theater receipts were tabulated at 230 million francs.[16] Even taking into account the inflation in France from 1923 to 1926, these figures reflect a steady growth in cinema attendance through the decade.

The figures were different for Germany. The trends were the same. The feebleness of the native film industry before 1914 and the catastrophe of national defeat and ensuing turmoil in 1918 did not prevent the movies from flourishing in Germany after World War I. By the end of 1919 there were already 2,836 movie theaters in Germany. In the following year alone some 700 new ones were opened. By 1929 the Reich counted 5,267 cinemas.[17] As quickly as the grand boulevards had become a center for plush movie theaters in Paris after 1918, a comparable district grew up around the Zoo Station in Berlin. The UFA Palast am Zoo, for example, opened with much fanfare and a silver fountain in front of its main entrance, and within several years a "Bier- und Wein-Keller" serving hundreds was opened in the cinema's basement. A stone's throw from the UFA Palast, customers streamed past marble columns into the equally large and comfortable Marmorhaus, and just up the street crowds flocked to the Filmbühne Wien. As the movie-theater building boom continued unabated through the first years of the decade, the area became crowded with cinemas. As late as 1922, two new, huge cinemas were opened in the district in a single week: the Alhambra on the Kurfürstendamm and the Primus-Palast in the Potsdammerstrasse. Each had an expensive concert organ and a large orchestra pit, and both featured lavish comfort and lush interior décors.[18]

By the early 1920s, including the some 20 grand movie palaces located around the Zoo area, there were over 300 cinemas in the city of Berlin. Together they annually employed more than 8,000 persons.[19] Apparently, however, those cinemas could not accommodate all the would-be movie-goers in the German capital. In 1920 the Berlin Sportspalast (formerly an auditorium for boxing matches and bicycle races and later a center for political rallies) was converted into a movie theater whose promoters claimed it to be the largest in the world.[20] But even capacity crowds at the Sportspalast were not half as large as the audiences numbering up to 22,000 that saw films presented at Berlin's open-air "Waldbühne" during the summer months.[21]

To the south, movie-going was so popular by 1919 that in Munich cinema admissions for the single month of July were greater than they had been for the entire year 1918.[22] In 1920 the Circus Schumann, located in the center of Frankfurt am Main, was purchased by the Decla-Bioscope company and converted into a 5,000-seat movie theater.[23] The symbolism of this business move should not be missed; it represented the waning of the circus, which had been nineteenth-century Europe's most popular mass entertainment, and its replacement by the cinema. From one end of Germany to the other, throughout the 1920s, the pattern persisted. The winter of 1926/27, for example, saw the opening of 7 new movie theaters in Hamburg alone, each with a seating capacity between 1,500 and 2,000.[24] In Germany the number of movie theaters with 600 to 1,000 seats doubled during the decade, while the number of those with more than 1,000 seats quadrupled.[25] By 1924 Berlin recorded over 40 million paid admissions to the cinemas,[26] and daily attendance at the movies throughout the Reich has risen to over 2 million.[27] This popularity of the cinema in Germany was not strictly an urban phenomenon. Throughout the 1920s some 50 to 60 per cent of Germany's movie-theater business was being done by cinemas (usually with about 300 seats each) located in the smaller cities and towns of the Reich.[28] In 1919 there were 12 cinema seats for every 1,000 inhabitants in Germany. Ten years later the ratio was 30 per 1,000.[29]

[21]

There were various indicators of the broad popularity of film during the 1920s. Early in the decade, specially designed cinema coaches in which movies were shown were being attached with increasing popularity to international express trains.[30] And movies took to the waves as well, as transatlantic liners vied for customers by offering the most popular "on board" film programs.[31] Film gained its first academic recognition in 1922 when the Paris Conservatory initiated courses in cinematography,[32] and in the same year the first serious archive for the preservation of motion pictures was founded in Germany.[33] The first film fair, which had been held in Leipzig, Germany, in March 1920, did not draw large crowds, but its failure to do so was attributed to the fact that its timing coincided with the abortive "Kapp Putsch," which caused temporary turmoil.[34] Subsequent efforts were more successful. National and international film fairs as well as various exhibitions and special shows devoted to cinematography became immensely popular during the 1920s.[35]

The popularity that cinema had attained in the 1920s did not, however, ensure sound and stable business conditions for the movie companies of France and Germany. On the contrary, movie-making was a high-risk venture, and the various branches of the industry were highly competitive. The French firm Pathé, founded in 1906 as a family enterprise, had by 1914 become an international undertaking.[36] Shortly after the end of World War I, however, the dismantling of Pathé's cinematographic imperium began. By 1919 Pathé's interests in Russia were lost to the Revolution, and her distribution firm in the United States had been sold to the Chase Bank of New York. The raw film plants in Jersey City owned by Pathé were purchased by the American company DuPont.[37] By the same year Pathé also had started to retrench at home. The firm began to de-emphasize film production in favor of film distribution and exploitation.[38] The process was complete by February 1921 when Pathé Cinema became the Pathé Consortium, abandoning film production.[39] The move was justified by Charles Pathé, who believed that the spiraling costs of feature-film production rendered film-making too risky.[40] Pathé owned a modest chain of movie theaters and concentrated on film rental and distribution, only occasionally loaning some capital to independent producers. Financially, the cautious policy seemed wise. Pathé showed steady profits through the twenties and was able to pay dividends of at least 10 per cent to stockholders with regularity.[41]

The history of Gaumont during the 1920s was similar, although the company did not abandon production entirely until 1925.[42] For the next few years it functioned mainly as a distribution firm in league with Hollywood's Metro-Goldwyn-Mayer.[43] Only in 1929 did Gaumont split with M-G-M, forming a new company called Gaumont Franco Film Aubert to make sound films.[44] A third French production company, Éclair Film, which, like Pathé and Gaumont, had established itself solidly before World War I, produced only two significant films after 1918. It gave up film production in 1924 to concentrate on the printing of positive film, equipment rental, and the leasing of studio space.[45]

Film historians have often pointed out that bankers and others of established wealth in France were reluctant to extend credit to film-makers during the 1920s.[46] Pathé and Gaumont, which had prospered in the days of the primitive one-reel movies before 1914, were naturally shy about embarking upon feature-film production for a new, mass audience. In the 1920s the family firm, "with its attachment to entrepreneurial independence," still predominated in France and seemed ill equipped to deal with the high risks of feature-film production.[47] Still, in some quarters the opinion prevailed that investment capital was available, but that it did not flow to film producers because of "their unsatisfactory ventures in the past."[48]

For all these difficulties, the descriptions of the French

cinema as having been in a constant state of chaos during the 1920s are exaggerated. For most of the decade France's annual production of feature films stood numerically fifth in the world, behind the United States, Japan, Germany, and the Soviet Union.[49] And this was no mean accomplishment. In comparison to all other European nations, "only in France was there a film industry with sufficient vigor to survive the twenties without governmental assistance."[50] This "vigor" was spread among a considerable number of independent producers.

One of these was Henri Diamant-Berger, an actor and director who turned producer in 1920 and oversaw the making of a number of box-office hits as well as the first films by René Clair.[51] Even more successful than Diamant-Berger was Louis Aubert, an ambitious film distributor who launched a small production firm at the end of World War I. Aubert earned a fortune with a 1921 production of *L'Atlantide* (directed by Jacques Feyder) and continued throughout the decade as a highly successful independent producer.[52] Film director René Plaissetty set up his own small production firm in 1919.[53] Some months later, the clever director of many a popular film, René Hervil, followed suit.[54] In 1923 a new production firm was founded with the announced intention of "transposing the history of France to the screen"; journalist André Antoine led the company's management.[55] Another newspaperman, Jean Sapène of *Le Matin*, formed the "Société des Cineromans," which produced serialized adventure films.[56] Ermolieff, a firm established by a group of Russian émigrés, successfully produced numerous films directed by their countrymen Victor Tourjansky and Alexandre Volkoff as well as by native Frenchmen.[57] And in 1924 another Russian living in Paris, Alexandre Kamenka, formed the surprisingly prolific production company called Films Albatros.[58] The most successful of the small production operations was, however, the team of Marcel Vandal (the founder of Éclair, who sold out and went independent) and Charles Delac.[59]

These small production companies often did not own studios, in which case production facilities were rented for each new film individually.[60] They did possess the connections for raising capital for each new movie, sometimes "overnight." And on occasions they joined forces for a big production, as when Louis Aubert teamed with Vandal and Delac in making the popular *La Bataille* (directed by E. E. Violet, 1923).[61] These small, independent companies did not account for all French feature-film production in the 1920s. Their efforts were supplemented by numerous firms "set up specifically to make a single picture," which were disbanded as soon as the film was completed.[62]

Small, independent, and "one-shot" producers characterized the French cinema of the 1920s. This did not mean, however, that every French film was a shoestring production. At times Henri Diamant-Berger complained that he could not find enough money to pay a scenario writer,[63] but when it came to his production of *Les Trois mousquetaires*, he managed to raise two million francs.[64] The Louis Aubert production of *L'Atlantide* was filmed almost entirely on location in North Africa and made handsome profits in spite of its "staggering" costs.[65] To support an entire film crew on location in a foreign country was a challenge that even Hollywood's richest producers did not undertake in the 1920s.[66] Money could be raised even in France for the "right" production.

The other branches of the film industry were like the production sector: characterized by small-scale enterprises that were highly competitive. Producer and distributor were usually not identical. Film distributors in France (called "éditeurs") usually purchased films outright from the producers and then bargained with movie-theater owners over rental contracts.[67] Block booking and blind booking, schemes for forcing theater owners to rent a "package" of films from the producer distributor—a practice already common in the United States—did not exist in France.[68] And although Pathé and Gaumont both owned movie-theater chains, during the 1920s 98 per cent of the cinemas in France were owned by individuals.[69]

The French cinema was characterized not only by a highly competitive, nonmonopolistic situation in every branch of the industry, but also by the government's policy of nonintervention in cinematographic affairs. Governmental aid to the film industry was limited to the commissioning of documentary, educational, and instructional films,[70] and the occasional technical assistance that governmental agencies might provide for the production of specific films.[71] These gestures were for all practical purposes meaningless. During the 1920s the French government did not financially support the film industry and apparently had no thoughts of doing so. A study completed for the Motion Picture Producers and Distributors of America at the end of the decade concluded that France was the only nation in Europe that would never subsidize its moviemakers.[72]

The situation in Germany was quite different. At the center of the German film industry was a firm called Universum Film A.G. ("UFA"). It came into being in midsummer 1917 when Field Marshal General Erich Ludendorff requested of the Ministry of War that the German film industry be unified. This he said was necessary to increase the number of entertainment films to be shown to troops as well as to home-front audiences, and to make propaganda film production more efficient.[73] The UFA quickly bought out several small film companies, including the Danish-owned Nordisk Film. The government itself provided one-third of the company's basic capital of 24 million marks, and the other shares were purchased by individual and corporate stockholders.[74] At the same time an agency called BUFA ("Bild- und Film-Amt") was established to manage cinemas for soldiers near the front and to collect photographic and cinematographic documents of the war.[75] With the proclamation of a German Republic on the ninth and

[26]

the ensuing armistice on the eleventh of November 1918, the BUFA was immediately demilitarized and was dismantled the following month.[76] The UFA, however, survived. The new regime, nominally Social Democrat and led by Friedrich Ebert, promptly acknowledged that the government held one-third of UFA's stock—information its predecessor had never publicized.[77] Having done that, it did nothing else. Amidst talk of socializing Germany's film industry,[78] the government failed to exert influence on the management of UFA.[79] A governmental report concluded in July 1919 that the UFA was operating just like any other capitalistic private enterprise.[80] The report was filed, and another irony of Weimar Germany's "republic without republicans" was let ride. And UFA rode tall in the saddle for the next several years. The firm showed handsome profits for 1919/20,[81] and for 1920/21 profits doubled to more than seven million marks.[82] For 1921/22 UFA paid dividends of 30 per cent to shareholders. Dividends for 1922/23 were still higher but meant little as money practically lost its value due to inflation. By the business year 1923/24 profits declined, as did dividends, which sank to 6 per cent.[83]

At the beginning of 1921 the German government published a pamphlet describing its financial investments and subsidies to German industry. It did not mention the holdings in UFA, an omission soon exposed by the film trade journal Der Film-Kurier.[84] Several months later, with no publicity, the government transferred its UFA shares to the Deutsche Bank, a private institution that had semiofficial status.[85] The amount of compensation received by the government apparently did not equal the real value of the stock, and the transaction being shrouded in secrecy was in principle inappropriate.

Besides the Deutsche Bank, a number of important German financial and industrial concerns held stock in UFA. Among them were AEG, HAPAG, Norddeutscher Lloyd, Henkel, Carl Lindstrom A.G. (Germany's largest manufacturer of phonograph records), the brokerage firms of Jacquier und Seaurius, and Schwarz, Goldschmidt, and Co., as well as the Dresdener Bank.[86] This impressive line-up of backers, however, did not ensure the UFA of sustained business success. By 1924, UFA was in the red.[87] In hopes of setting UFA's house in order, a prominent banker, Dr. Ferdinand Bausbach, was named general director of the firm. During the first year of his tenure, UFA lost 50 million marks. In the middle of that disastrous business year, 1925/26, UFA entered a contract with the Hollywood companies Metro-Goldwyn-Mayer and Famous Players–Lasky Corporation. They each extended two million dollars to UFA at a 7½ per cent interest rate, and UFA agreed to distribute in the Reich certain films produced by M-G-M and Famous that those firms considered "suitable for the German market."[88] At the same time, the Prussian Ministry for Science, Fine Arts, and Education began a series of loans to UFA through its documentary film subsidiary Deulig. These loans continued through 1928.[89] Still, UFA's financial woes were not solved. Early in 1927 competition began between three companies, the Ullstein-Konzern, the Mosse-Konzern, and the Hugenberg-Konzern, for purchase of controlling shares in UFA.[90] In April of that year Alfred Hugenberg, a publisher and nationalist political figure (D.N.V.P.), purchased the largest single block of UFA stock.[91] Ludwig Klitzsch, a trusted Hugenberg colleague, became general director of UFA.[92] He moved quickly to pay off the loans from M-G-M and Famous, hence releasing UFA from contractural obligations to the Hollywood firms.[93] This process completed, Hugenberg boasted that his actions had served "to maintain for German interests a totally worthwhile German cultural institution."[94]

For the purposes of this study, two questions should be asked about UFA's activities during the 1920s. First, did UFA monopolize the German film industry? Second, did the shares held in UFA by the government, and later by the

Hugenberg-Konzern, translate in either or both cases into an ideological influence on feature-film production? On the first question, the documentation does not support the claim that UFA monopolized German film production. Consider the following chart for the last half of the decade:[95]

Year	German Feature Films	UFA Produced	Percent of Total UFA
1926	185	12	6.5
1927	242	15	6.2
1928	224	16	7.1
1929	183	13	7.1

Other statistics are equally revealing on this point. At the end of World War I there were 131 film-producing companies in Germany; by 1920 there were 230. The count reached 360 in 1922, and at the end of the decade there were 424 film-production companies in the Reich.[96] In an average year during the 1920s, one-quarter of Germany's feature-length films were produced by companies that in a given year made only one film. Another 50 per cent of the feature films were made by small companies that produced between two and five films per year. Normally, around 7 per cent of the annual feature production was from UFA and the remaining films were turned out by several other large firms such as Emelka, Phoebus, and so forth.[97] Many of the most expensive films shown in Germany during the period were produced by UFA, which did not necessarily mean they were box-office successes, though some were. On the whole, features made by independent and small producers competed in popularity with the movies made by UFA and other large companies.[98]

UFA earned much of its revenue from nonproduction sources, such as the rental of studio space and equipment.[99] The firm was also very active in film rental and distribution and owned its own chain of movie theaters. Still, film distribution and rental was nearly as competitive in Germany as it was in France; the monopolistic practices of "block booking" and "blind booking" were unknown.[100] Though UFA owned Europe's largest chain of movie houses, even by the end of the decade it linked only 74 cinemas. Germany's second largest film company, Emelka, owned 50 movie theaters by 1929.[101] Together, these two chains accounted for less than 3 per cent of the over 5,000 movie theaters in the German Reich.[102]

Production at UFA was divided between four departments that had nothing to do with each other. They were: (1) documentary films and Deulig production, (2) the publicity and advertising film division, (3) weekly newsreel production, known as *Wochenschau*, and (4) feature-film production.[103] The UFA was neither monopolistic nor monolithic. It was a cartel linking a number of firms, subsidiaries, and branches in what were loose corporate relationships.[104]

From the end of 1918 through 1921, when the German Republic nominally held one-third of UFA's stock, there is no evidence of governmental intervention in the firm's affairs. Notably, government representatives did not even exercise voting rights on the basis of its shares. In this period UFA produced just four films under government contract. Two of them were apolitical: *Die weisse Seuche* was about the dangers of tuberculosis, and *Krüppelnot und Krüppelhilfe* was an informational film about artificial limbs and therapy for amputees. In May 1919 the regime did finance a short film about the Allied blockage of Germany, *Die Folgen der Hungerblockade*.[105] And in April 1920 it commissioned an anti-Bolshevik "documentary" through UFA. When the film, entitled *Der schwarze Gott*, was ready for distribution, the government became reluctant to honor its original commitment to the project. It considered banning the film and then chose to let it be shown, but discouraged its becoming popular.[106] The irony of the government's indifference to UFA was emphasized in the summer of 1919 when the regime launched production of a short film entitled Die Sozialisierung Marschiert (Socialization Marches On). The contract was not given to UFA in which the government held stock, but to an independent, privately owned film company.[107]

More surprising, perhaps, was that the nationalist political figure Hugenberg showed scant interest in influencing UFA feature-film production. Erich Pommer, who had been in charge of the feature-film division at UFA since the beginning of the decade and had left the firm shortly before Hugenberg moved to "rescue" it in April 1927, was promptly recalled to that post.[108] Thus, the Hugenberg "takeover" served to restore the dominance of the independent-minded Pommer. The most complete study of Hugenberg's role in the UFA, by Valeska Dietrich, concludes that any inclination he might have had to impose his ideology on UFA feature films was sacrificed to business considerations. The UFA policy after 1927 was simple: "The firm would have to gear itself to the production of films which would fill the cash register."[109] Hugenberg was a man of the press. It is questionable if he conceived of feature films as vehicles for political messages. He did, however, recognize the weekly UFA newsreel as a source of public information similar to his own daily newspapers. After 1927 there was no marked change in the content of the feature films turned out by Pommer's division of UFA, but the weekly newsreels became increasingly slanted, emphasizing German nationalist viewpoints and interpretation of events.[110]

From time to time the German government did extend subsidies and loans to several film companies during the 1920s.[111] And it turned out that state funds supported a film firm called Phoebus without the regime knowing it. The case was bizarre. In 1923 Phoebus was founded and opened its own studios in Berlin.[112] In the spring of 1924, the com-

[31]

pany launched a distribution division.[113] By 1926 Phoebus had become a leader in German feature-film production, making nine movies that year.[114] In 1927 it went bankrupt. It was then discovered that the mastermind behind Phoebus was an army captain named Lohmann, and that from the beginning most of the firm's financing was done with secret funds of the Reichswehr. It was finally determined that the sum used for these purposes was more than 20 million marks.[115] The firm was liquidated, and Minister of War Otto Gessler was forced to resign as a result of these revelations.[116] No evidence was uncovered to indicate that the Phoebus venture was more than a money-making scheme based on the principle of embezzlement. The only suggestion that any Phoebus films portrayed a particular ideological line came in a complaint from the Federation of Austrian Army Officers addressed to the German government in January 1928. The group claimed that two Phoebus-produced films, *Leichte Kavallerie* and *Bundesgenossen*, had portrayed the Austrian army as composed of cowardly incompetents.[117]

There is no evidence that governmental investment and the backing of important German capitalists had any direct influence on the content of German feature films in the 1920s. This backing did permit the production of some grandiose and artistically pretentious films in the period. While these particular films in their plots followed formulas common to films popular in Germany, it was known that they were also potentially popular in other countries.[118] The techniques used in these films were "avant-garde," often employing expressionistic sets, imaginative lighting, and creative camera work. But their story lines were not avant-garde at all. This was explainable because of the limited sense in which German film-makers perceived the value of the feature film as propaganda. After World War I Germany was a pariah nation whose image needed improving. These monumental, "artistic" films could appeal to the mass, national audience for their plots and still draw worldwide critical acclaim for their cinematographic techniques.[119] The real propaganda function of the German film in this period was the attempt to draw favorable foreign attention to the talents of her filmmakers with certain productions.

During the 1920s both the French and the German film industries operated in relatively free markets. The monopolistic practices in film production, distribution, and exploitation that already existed in the United States had not yet taken hold.[120] UFA was not a monopoly, and for much of the decade the company was being run at a loss. Movie-making is a high-risk venture, and the history of the film industry everywhere bears this out. In France there was great concern during the period over that country's lack of large-scale production firms. But the "crisis" of the decade was not unique. As Jacques Durand wrote in 1958 with complete accuracy, the film industry in France had been in a perpetual state of crisis "for the last fifty years."[121] In the cinema, success is fickle. France produced barely half as many films per year as Germany in the 1920s. But after 1930 France annually produced more films than Germany in every year right up to the eve of World War II.

In both countries the film producer had to compete for the largest possible portion of the mass, national audience. That audience was in no way definable by class, age, sex, or geography. Testimony from the period is reinforced by a general description of the national patterns of movie-going. The most successful films were those that appealed to the broadest cross section of the population as a whole. The most prosperous film-makers were those who could manage to keep turning out new films that appealed to the collective taste of the mass, national audience. And this was no easy business, as the sketch of the film industry in both France and Germany during the 1920s reveals.

NOTES

1. *Le Courrier cinématographique*, 9 ème année, no. 18, 3 May 1919, p. 32.
2. Typescript copy, Conference on "Le Cinéma devant la société," Idhec, Paris, 5 December 1944. Opening remarks by Pierre Bost. Copy of the Library of Idhec, Paris.
3. Jacques Chastenet, *Les Années d'illusions, 1918–1939* (Paris: 1960), p. 20.
4. In many sources, including the three cited above, the popularity of the movies right after World War I is attributed to "war weariness."
5. Maurice Bardech and Robert Brasillach, *Histoire du cinéma* (Paris: 1965), I, p. 13. The point is argued among film historians, with some coming down on the side of the argument that the war hastened technical developments in cinematography and the growth of the movies' popularity.
6. J. Shige Suduzy, "Cinema in Japan," *Close-up*, vol. IV, no. 2, February 1929, p. 22. For most of the 1920s Japan had the second most productive film industry in the world.
7. Jacques Durand, "Le Film, est-il une marchandise?" *Le Cinéma, fait social*, XXVIIème semaine sociale universitaire, 20–25 April 1959, p. 34.
8. G.-Michel Coissac, *Histoire du cinématographe* (Paris: 1925), p. 361. See also Jacques Brunius, *En Marge du cinéma français* (Paris: 1954), pp. 56 ff.
9. Coissac, *op. cit.*, pp. 362–4.
10. *La Cinématographie française*, 2ème année, no. 24, 19 April 1919, p. 35.
11. *La Cinématographie française*, 14ème année, 23 August 1923, pp. 17, 18, and *op. cit.*, 30 August 1924, pp. 25, 26. For a district by district breakdown on cinemas in Paris, see Le Courrier cinématographique. 9éme année. no. 27. 4 July 1919, p. 8. Other documentation on the movie theaters in France is found in *La Cinématographie française*, 7ème année, no. 355, 22 August 1925, p. 10 and *op. cit.*, no. 358, 12 September 1925, p. 11.
12. Jacques Durand, *Le Cinéma et son public* (Paris: 1958), p. 91.
13. *La Cinématographie française*, 2ème année, no. 4, 25 January 1919, pp. 79, 80; *op. cit.*, no. 6, no date, p. 76; *op. cit.*, no. 8, p. 62. During 1919 the journal *La Cinématographie française* ran a series on movie-theater building and refurbishing in France under the title "Le Tour de France projectionniste." See also *Le Courrier cinématographique*, 10ème année, no. 3, 17 January 1920, pp. 6, 15, and *op. cit.*, 9ème année, no. 30, 26 July 1919, p. 8.

14. La Cinématographie française, 2ème année, no. 16, 22 February 1919, p. 63.
15. Paul Leglise, Histoire de la politique du cinéma français: "Le Cinéma et la IIIème republique" (Paris: 1970), p. 55.
16. André Chevanne, L'Industrie du cinéma (Bordeaux: 1933), p. 77.
17. Friedrich Zgliniki, Der Weg des deutschen Films (Frankfurt a.M.: 1955), p. 328.
18. Alexander Jason, Jahrbuch der Filmindustrie (Berlin: 1923), I, pp. 126–31; Mario Kenner, Berlin im Wandel des Jahrhunderts (Berlin: 1956), p. 253. Die Lichtbildbühne, 12. Jahrg., no. 48, 29 November 1919, p. 21. See the UFA Records, Package R 109, Section 76 for a copy of the concessionaire's license for the UFA Palast am Zoo. Der Kinematograph, 16. Jahrg., no. 145, 5 March 1922, no page number.
19. Revue Internationale du cinéma educateur, 2ème année, no. 1, January 1930, p. 11.
20. See various issues of the journal Der Film-Kurier for 1920 and 1921.
21. Zgliniki, op. cit., p. 339.
22. Der Kinematograph, 13. Jahrg., no. 657, 6 August 1919, p. 26.
23. Der Film-Kurier, 2. Jahrg., no. 148, 9 July 1920, p. 1.
24. Le Courrier cinématographique, 18ème année, no. 6, 5 February 1927, p. 10.
25. Peter Bächlin, Der Film als Ware (Basel: 1947), p. 51.
26. Kurt Wesse, Grossmacht Film (Berlin: 1928), p. 25. See also the pamphlet Die deutsche Filmindustrie unter dem deutschen Reichstag, 1927, in the Bundesarchiv Koblenz under "Sackgruppe: Presse."
27. Walter Plugge, Film und Gesetzgebung (Berlin: 1924), no page number. Daily attendance in France at the same time was estimated at just over one million; see Durand, Le Cinema et son public, p. 209. It was considered, however, that the daily attendance in France was actually higher, and that reporting methods there were more primitive than in Germany, which accounted for the low figures.
28. Karl Wolffsohn, Jahrbuch der Filmindustrie (Berlin: 1930), IV, p. 312.
29. H. H. Wollenberg, Fifty Years of German Film (London: 1948), pp. 15, 16.
30. Der Film-Kurrier, 6. Jahrg., no. 71, 22 March 1924, p. 1.
31. Zgliniki, op. cit., p. 329.
32. Auguste Nardy, "Le Cinéma au conservatoire," Bonsoir (Paris), 14 January 1922, p. 3.
33. Der Kinematograph, 17. Jahrg., nos. 828/829, 7 January 1923, pp. 23, 24. This archive, however, was private, having been founded by an independent film club. The first state film archive was established in Germany in 1935. In France during the 1920s various governmental ministries preserved copies of documentary films they had commissioned. During the 1930s, Henri Langlois began the collection that became the basis of the Cinémathèque français holdings.

34. Jason, op. cit., p. 37.
35. Karl Lütge, "Der Verlauf des Leipziger Kino- und Photo-Messe," Der Kinematograph, 16. Jahrg., no. 811, 3 September 1922, pp. 1–3.
36. Coissac, op. cit., pp. 468 ff.
37. Jean Mitry, Index Historique du cinéma (Paris: 1967), p. 129.
38. Le Courrier cinématographique, 9ème année, no. 28, 12 July 1919, p. 2.
39. Jean Mitry, Index Historique du cinéma, p. 135.
40. Jason, op. cit., p. 32. In 1917 an average film cost about $1,000. By 1920 the average cost of a feature film was already between $40,000 and $80,000 and rising. See the discussion in Durand, "Le Film, est-il une marchandise," pp. 31 ff.
41. Jàson, op. cit., p. 25.
42. Zgliniki, op. cit., p. 412.
43. Jean Mitry, Index Historique du cinéma, p. 143. And René Jeanne and Charles Ford, Histoire encyclopédique du cinéma (Paris: 1947), I, p. 485.
44. Jean Mitry, Index Historique du cinéma, p. 156.
45. See Coissac, op. cit., pp. 502–5.
46. Jean Felix, Le Chemin du cinéma (Paris: 1934), p. 15. Also, André Chevanne, op. cit., p. 45, and Georges Sadoul, Histoire du cinéma français (Paris: 1962), p. 23.
47. See David S. Landes, The Unbound Prometheus (Cambridge: 1969), pp. 245, 526, 527. While it cannot be demonstrated conclusively that film firms like Pathé and Gaumont fell into the pattern of family-run businesses that Landes describes, there are several indications that the firms' activities conformed to his model.
48. Howard Lewis, The Motion Picture Industry (New York: 1933), p. 416.
49. Léon Moussinac, Panoramique du cinéma (Paris: 1958), p. 17. Also, Wollenberg, op. cit., and Jacob Wolffsohn, Jahrbuch der Filmindustrie (Berlin: 1928), III, p. 432.
50. Arthur Knight, The Liveliest Art (New York and Toronto: 1957), p. 93.
51. La Cinématographie française, no. 97, 11 September 1920, p. 89. For further information on Diamant-Berger, see Jason, op. cit., p. 35. Also based on my unpublished interview with Henri Diamant-Berger in Paris, 1971.
52. Pierre Leprohon, Cinquante Ans du cinéma français (Paris: 1954), p. 56. Also, Coissac, op. cit., pp. 492 ff.
53. La Cinématographie française, no. 35, 5 July 1919, p. 39.
54. La Cinématographie française, nos. 71, 72, and 73 réunis, 3 April 1920, p. 33.
55. L'Astigmate, "Petite Chronique de l'écran," Bonsoir (Paris), 2 September 1923, p. 3.
56. Sadoul, op. cit., p. 44. Also, Mitry, Index Historique du cinéma, pp. 142, 143, and Coissac, op. cit., p. 479.

57. Leprohon, *op. cit.*, p. 80.
58. Sadoul, *op. cit.*, p. 46. For a description of some of the production activity of the Films Albatros, see Pierre Leprohon, *Jean Epstein* (Paris: 1964), p. 39.
59. Coissac, *op. cit.*, p. 502.
60. Pathé, Gaumont, and Eclair made sizable profits on rental of such facilities to "one-shot" producers during the period.
61. The film itself is identified as a Vandal-Delac production "in conjunction with" Louis Aubert.
62. Knight, *op. cit.*, p. 93.
63. *Bonsoir* (Paris), 12 July 1923, p. 3.
64. André Lang, *Déplacements et villégiatures littéraires* (Paris: no date), p. 116.
65. Pierre Leprohon, *L'Exotisme et le cinéma* (Paris: 1945), p. 113.
66. Sending an entire film crew on location was not all that rare in France during the 1920s. See, for example, Kevin Brownlow, *The Parade's Gone By* (London 1969), pp. 537, 538, and *La Petite Illustration*, no. 7, 7 August 1926, p. 5.
67. Henri Fescourt, *et al.*, *Le Cinéma: des origines à nos jours* (Paris: 1932), pp. 162, 163.
68. Bächlin, *op. cit.*, pp. 39, 40.
69. Walter Dadek, *Die Filmwirtschaft* (Freiburg: 1957), p. 21.
70. *La Cinématographie française*, no. 9, 4 January 1919, p. 59.
71. See for example, R. M., "Un Grand film francais, La Bataille," *Ciné-Miroir*, 3ème année, no. 45, 1 March 1924, p. 72.
72. Lewis, *op. cit.*, p. 416.
73. Otto Kriegk, *Der deutsche Film im Spiegel der UFA* (Berlin: 1943), p. 61; Fritz Olimsky, *Tendenzen der Filmwirtschaft und deren Auswirkung auf die Filmpresse*, unpublished dissertation, Friedrich Wilhelm Universität, Berlin, 1931, p. 24.
74. UFA Records, Package R 109, Section 139, copy of the purchase contract of the "Nordisk Film Kompagnie, Kopenhagen," which had an extensive operation in Germany. Bundesarchiv, Koblenz.
75. Zgliniki, *op. cit.*, p. 363.
76. Jason, *op. cit.*, p. 28.
77. Siegfried Kracauer, *From Caligari to Hitler* (Princeton: 1947), p. 36, claims that the government renounced its shares in UFA after the armistice in November, 1918. Kracauer cites as his source on this point Alexander Jason, *Jahrbuch der Filmindustrie* (Berlin: 1923), I, p. 28, which, in fact, does not corroborate the claim.
78. Walter Thielemann, "Die Sozialisierung der Lichtspieltheater," *Der Kinematograph*, 13. Jahrg, no. 656, 30 July 1919, pp. 19, 20. Also, *Der Film*, 4. Jahrg., no. 16, 19 April 1919, p. 27, and Jason, *op. cit.*, p. 28. Only in Kurt Eisner's Bavaria were steps actually taken to socialize the theater and the cinema; see *Die Lichtbildbühne*, 12. Jahrg., no. 15, 12 April 1919, pp. 1, 2. A movement to "communalize" the movie theaters by putting them under municipal

ownership came to a vote in the Reichstag in 1920 and failed by only a small margin. See the *Deutsche Lichtspiel-Zeitung*, 8. Jahrg., no. 1, 3 January 1920, pp. 1, 2, and *ibid.*, no. 19, 8 May 1920, pp. 1–4.

79. UFA Records, Package R 109, Section 77, Geschäftsbericht der Universum Film Aktiengesellschaft für die Geschäftsjahre 1918, 1919, und das Zwischengeschäftsjahr vom 1. Januar bis 31. Mai 1920, Bundesarchiv, Koblenz. In the period covered, although the old regime fell and was replaced by a republican government, there was not a single change in UFA's board of directors.

80. Bericht an den Herrn Unterstaatssekretär in der Reichskanzlei von der Reichsfilmstelle über die Universum Film A.G., 26 July 1919, Folio 1–298, R 431/2497, pp. 30, 31, Bundesarchiv Koblenz.

81. UFA Records, Package R 109, 60/301, Section 85, Bundesarchiv Koblenz.

82. Letter from UFA to Herrn Oskar Meester, 15 March 1922, in UFA Records, Package R 109, 6/301, Section 85, Bundesarchiv Koblenz.

83. Hans Traub, *Fünf-und-Zwanzig Jahre UFA* (Berlin: 1942), p. 59.

84. *Der Film-Kurier*, 3. Jahrg., no. 52, 2 March 1921, p. 1.

85. H. P. Manz, *UFA und der frühe deutsche Film* (Zurich: 1963), p. 11.

86. Klaus-Dieter Bärthel. *Die Rolle der Universum Film A.G. bei der ideologischen Beeinflussung der Massen im Sinne der reaktionärsten Krafte des deutschen Monopolkapitals und ihrer aggressiven Pläne, 1918 bis 1933*, unpublished dissertation, Karl Marx Universität, Leipzig, 1965, pp. 30, 31.

87. Valeska Dietrich, *Alfred Hugenberg: Ein Manager in der Publizistik*, unpublished Dissertation, Freie Universität, West Berlin, 1960, p. 41.

88. Bärthel, *op. cit.*, pp. 17, 18. The original contract is to be found in UFA Records, Package R 109, Section 121, Bundesarchiv Koblenz. On UFA's side the promissory notes were guaranteed by the Bank für Grundbesitz und Handel A.G., an UFA subsidiary.

89. UFA Records, Package R 109, Section 155 contain several letters and communiqués between the company and the Preussischer Minister für Wissenschaft, Kunst und Volksbildung. See also Auszug aus dem Protokoll der Sitzung des Reichministeriums vom 31. January 1927, RK 655, Folio 1–269, R 431/2499, p. 5. Both in the Bundesarchiv Koblenz.

90. Dietrich, *op. cit.*, p. 41.

91. Kriegk, *op. cit.*, pp. 122, 123.

92. Dietrich, *op. cit.*, p. 41. Klitzsch had established himself in Hugenberg's confidence as director of the Scherl Verlag, which was one of Hugenberg's holdings.

93. Kreigk, *op. cit.*, pp. 122, 123.

94. Zgliniki, *op. cit.*, p. 420.

95. Bärthel, *op. cit.*, p. 19.

96. Wollenberg, *op. cit.*, pp. 15–17.

97. Olimsky, *op. cit.*, p. 12.

98. Producers for German silent films can be established by referring to Gerhard Lamprecht, *Deutsche Stummfilme* (Berlin 1965–71), 8 vols. Among the most successful producers of films were a group of independently operating Jewish businessmen who were known as the "Friedrichstrasse Group," as reported in David Stewart Hull, *Film in the Third Reich* (Berkeley and Los Angeles: 1969), p. 23. Also, for example, the director of the earliest and most successful of the "Mountaineering films," Dr. Arnold Fanck, raised capital privately for these film projects until the bigger firms caught on to the popularity of the genre. Fanck comments on this in a letter to Klaus Kreimeier at the Deutsche Kinemathek dated 24 April 1972.

99. Wolffsohn, *op. cit.*, p. 200. Various contracts between UFA and other firms (both German and foreign) for the rental of production facilities and space are found in the UFA Records, Package R 109, Section 76, Bundesarchiv Koblenz.

100. Bächlin, *op. cit.*, pp. 39, 40. Again, the UFA Records, Package R 109, Section 100 contain pertinent documents. Rental agreements for films between UFA (as producer) and independent theaters never indicate any "blind" or "block" booking system.

101. Letter from Vertretung der Reichsregierung in München to the Reichskanzlei, Berlin, 6 August 1929 reporting on theaters owned by Emelka (Münchener Lichtspielkunst, A.G.), in Folio 1–287, R 431/2498, p. 106, Bundesarchiv Koblenz.

102. In 1929 there were 5,267 movie theaters in the German Reich. See Zgliniki, *op. cit.*, p. 328; Felix, *op. cit.*, p. 80, and others.

103. Dietrich, *op. cit.*, p. 62.

104. The strongest claim that UFA was a monopoly is found in Bardech and Brasillach, *op. cit.*, p. 183. A concise summary of the interpretations of UFA's role in German film in the era is found in George Huaco, *The Sociology of Film Art* (New York and London: 1965), pp. 30 ff.

105. Aus dem Protokoll der Sitzung des Reichsministeriums vom Montag, den 26. Mai 1919, Folio 1–298, R 431/2497, p. 4, Bundesarchiv Koblenz. The UFA-made film, *Die Ruhrschande* (1923) was likely produced in part by state funds, though this cannot be proved conclusively; see letter from UFA to Staatssekretär Hamm in der Reichskanzlei, Folio 1–287, R 434/2498, p. 112, Bundesarchiv Koblenz.

106. Letter, Staatssekretär in der Reichskanzlei to the Reichsminister der Justiz, den Preussischen Minister des Innern, und den Staatskommissar für die öffentliche Ordnung, 24 February 1921, Folio 1–287, R 431/2498, p. 8, Bundesarchiv Koblenz.

107. *Regierung und Film* (Privatdruck in Berlin, 12 September 1919), p. 143, in Folio 1–298, R 431/2497, Bundesarchiv Koblenz.

108. Manz, *op. cit.*, p. 17. Olimsky, *op. cit.*, pp. 29, 30, in particular, points out that Hugenberg never expected people at UFA—

especially the "Fachleute"—to share his political views and represent them in film. See also Kracauer, *op. cit.*, p. 36. Even Bärthel, *op.
cit.*, at no point demonstrates that Hugenberg interferred with UFA
feature-film content before 1933. Interesting in this regard are interviews with Erich Pommer, reported in Huaco, *op. cit.*, p. 36, and
elsewhere.

109. Dietrich, *op. cit.*, pp. 79–81.
110. *Ibid.*, pp. 79–81.
111. The government moved in 1928 to keep foreign interests from buy-
ing shares in Emelka by investing in the firm. See Auszug aus dem
Protokoll der Ministerbesprechung, 10 November 1928, Folio
1–269, R 431/2499, p. 155, Bundesarchiv Koblenz. Reported at the
time in the *Berliner Tagesblatt* (Berlin), 15 November 1928, p. 1. The
subsidy for Emelka and the possibility of aiding other German film
companies were discussed in a communiqué from the Reichsminister des Innern to Der Staatssekretär in der Reichskanzlei, 16 July
1925, Folio 1–287, R 431/2498, pp. 203–5, Bundesarchiv Koblenz.
112. *Der Kinematograph*, 17. Jahrg., nos. 867/868, 7 October 1923, p. 2.
113. *Der Film-Kurier*, 6. Jahrg., no. 97, 24 April 1924, p. 5.
114. *Le Courrier cinématographique*, 18ème année, no. 9, 26 February
1927, p. 9.
115. *Ibid.*, 19ème année, no. 10, 10 March 1928, p. 54.
116. Gessler had taken the post of Minister of War shortly after the unsuccessful "Kapp Putsch" of 1920. He was considered a democrat and
supporter of the Republic. Kracauer, *op. cit.*, suggests in his version
of the Phoebus incident that it was used by conservatives to discredit
Gessler and force his dismissal. S. William Halperin's *Germany
Tried Democracy* (New York: 1946), pp. 356, 357, portrays Gessler
not so much as a victim of political enemies but as a man who had to
pay the price rightly for the numerous financial irregularities discovered in the use of the Reichswehr funds during his tenure as Minister of War.
117. Official communiqué from the Österreichischer Offiziers-Verband
Wien to the Deutscher Offizierbund, 13 January 1928, Folio 1–269, R
431/2499, pp. 102–4, Bundesarchiv Koblenz.
118. Kracauer, *op. cit.*, pp. 101 ff.
119. *Le Courrier cinématographique*, 10ème année, no. 17, 3 July 1920, p.
5. Kracauer, *op. cit.*, p. 37, seems to misinterpret UFA's interest in
foreign markets. See Huaco, *op. cit.*, p. 36, and elsewhere for Erich
Pommer's contribution on the matter.
120. Practices in the United States are described in Henri Mercillon,
Cinéma et monopoles (Paris: 1953).
121. Jacques Durand, *Le Cinéma et son public* (Paris: 1958), p. 1.

Film and
Governmental
Policy

The relationship between the government and the cinema in both France and Germany, respectively, during the 1920s developed around three issues. These were: (1) governmental policy on the import of foreign films, (2) the question of entertainment taxes levied on movie-theater admissions, and (3) the censorship of films by authorities.

A silent film could be easily and cheaply prepared for foreign distribution; this required only the substitution of new titles in a foreign language for the originals.[1] The boom in movie-going worldwide right after World War I encouraged the international trade in films. The international trade in films, in turn, prompted native film producers in various countries to urge their respective governments to limit film imports. During the 1920s this was the case in both France and Germany. The issue, however, was a complicated one. While producers favored official "protectionism" for their movies, not all elements in the film business agreed that foreign-film imports should be curtailed. Film rental agents and distributors who imported the foreign films were naturally opposed to such limitations. To this relatively small group was added the large number of independent movie-theater owners who also took a stand against the restriction of foreign-film imports. This conflict reflected, indeed, the highly competitive situation in the business in both countries. The availability of foreign films for rental translated into increased "bargaining power" for the cinema owners in dealing with distributors and rental agents. As a result, the film trade journals in both countries, whose readership consisted mainly of movie-theater proprietors, adopted editorial stands against importation quotas on foreign films.

In France the debate over foreign-film imports was already raging in 1919, but a proposal for legislation to limit such imports did not surface until 1922. In that year the "Groupe de Defense des Films Français" urged the National Assembly to adopt a law setting a tax of 20 per cent of a film's value on every foreign movie imported into France.[2] Instead, the lawmakers adopted a tariff of two francs per meter for any foreign film entering France. This was hardly the tax of 20 per cent of value that had been requested, and the tariff did little to discourage the import of films.[3] Thus, at the beginning of 1923 the French Society of Film Authors (i.e., scenario writers) proposed that the government establish a quota system for foreign-film imports to be based on the number of feature films the French industry produced annually.[4] This sort of quota legislation was commonly called a "contingent system" in film circles during the twenties. The French government moved slowly on the matter. At the beginning of 1928 a governmental "Commission Supérieure de Cinématographie," presided over by Edouard Herriot, presented a list of proposed reforms dealing with the cinema.[5] The most significant of

[42]

these established a policy of issuing a special license for each foreign film imported into France. The Parisian daily *L'Ami du Peuple* called the new policy a fake designed to skirt a real quota system.[6] The newspaper was correct. The Herriot decree established only that importation licenses would be issued or not issued following guidelines for "the conservation of national morals and traditions."[7] This was no quota law, but rather censorship legislation exposing foreign films to "double jeopardy." The National Censorship Board (which functioned under Herriot's Ministry of Education and Fine Arts) already had the power to ban any film it considered injurious to national morals or traditions. The second major proposal of Herriot's decree of February 1928 was also meaningless. It stipulated that countries exporting films to France would henceforth be "forced" to purchase French-produced films. The proposal was unworkable. For a time the French government did attempt to negotiate with its German counterpart, hoping to increase the export of French films to Germany. But this came to naught, and it was the last that was heard of the "enforcement clause" of Herriot's decree.[8] France adopted a "contingent law" based on a quota system in 1931, but so many exceptions to it were allowed that it scarcely functioned.[9] A more workable quota system for foreign films was briefly in effect in 1936 under the Popular Front government.[10]

In Germany, the split between film-producing interests and theater owners on this issue was as wide as in France. Since UFA, the largest German film producer, was, for a while, government subsidized, and since important business interests and banks eventually invested heavily in the film industry, it might have been expected that pressure on the government to limit foreign-film imports would have been more effective in Germany. But for the first few years after World War I German government officials feared that Germany could not afford such restrictions. The reasoning was that only by permitting foreign nations access to German markets could Germany hope to see an end to the boycott of her own goods in foreign lands.[11] Like so many other cinematographic matters during the 1920s, the German government's policy on restricting foreign-film imports was perceived in terms of general foreign policy. In September 1920 Germany adopted a "loose" and "flexible" quota system to limit foreign film imports.[12] "Loose" it was indeed. When in the first quarter of 1921 Italian film exports to Germany had already gone beyond the quota for the entire year, the German Foreign Ministry noted that this was a "special case," and the importation of Italian films continued.[13] Alas, almost every case seemed special; exceptions to the decree of 1920 were the rule. Foreign films continued to enter Germany unhindered. In January 1922, however, the Reich's Minister of the Economy issued an unexpected ban on all foreign films, arguing that they were a menace to the "infant" German film industry.[14] The Minister had acted on his own, and much to the dismay of the Foreign Ministry, which wanted to pursue a general policy of improving trade with other countries. In a matter of days the ban was rescinded.

The film-producing interests, however, finally carried the day.[15] On January 1, 1925 a "Film-Kontingentgesetz" went into effect in Germany. According to this law a foreign film could be imported into Germany only after the foreign distributor had purchased a permit ("Kontingentschein") from a German production firm, which was entitled to such a "Schein" after it had produced a new film.[16] In practice the law was a failure. Forging and blackmarketing of the permits was common.[17] Loopholes in the law were numerous, and the provisions for enforcement were vague.[18] Actually, the importation of foreign films into Germany increased steadily while the law was in effect.[19] It was abandoned in 1928, with protest from no one save representatives of the Bavarian State government, who argued unconvincingly that any foreign film was a threat to German culture.[20]

[44]

Attempts in both France and Germany to deal with film imports were ineffectual. The German government reacted more forcefully on the issue, but in the long run this made little difference. Much the same pattern characterized developments in regard to taxes on movie-theater admissions during the 1920s.

In December 1916 France had set national taxes on cinema admissions as follows:

5 percent on monthly cinema receipts up to 25,000 francs
10 percent "   "   "   "   " of 25–50,000 francs
20 percent "   "   "   "   " of 50–100,000 francs
25 percent "   "   "   "   " over 100,000 francs

Shortly after the war the National Assembly, responsive to the owners of legitimate theaters and music halls, increased the rates to 10 per cent on receipts up to 15,000 francs and 15 per cent on monthly receipts between 15,000 and 50,000 thousand francs.[21] By order of the Minister of Finance the rates were increased again in early 1920. Those increases were written into a new law of June 25, 1920 along with authorization for French municipalities to levy taxes on cinema admissions as they wished.[22] The result was that by 1921 cinemas in some French cities and towns were paying up to 75 per cent of the total taxes on admissions to local governments.[23] At the beginning of 1922 movie-theater owners in Paris and the surrounding area threatened to close their cinemas unless taxes were reduced.[24] The threat did not materialize, although one Parisian newspaper speculated that some two hundred movie theaters were forced to close during 1922 because they could not keep up the payment of high entertainment taxes.[25] In June 1923 a new law, intended to benefit small and middle-sized cinemas, readjusted the tax rates on movie-theater admissions.[26]

The government, however, refused to take action on local taxes. The film industry quickly realized that reform in this area would be slow and piecemeal. During the first six months of 1924 agitation against local entertainment taxes increased markedly throughout France. The common means was a strike or threatened strike by the movie-theater owners in a town or city. The results varied. Boulogne-sur-Mer raised its taxes in response to a strike by the movie-theater owners,[27] and a magistrate in Levallois-Perret reacted to a strike threat by cinema owners with pique and anger.[28] But most municipalities reacted in a spirit of compromise, and local taxes on movie admissions were reduced. By 1928 the total tax (national and local) on cinema receipts in Paris ranged between 17 and 40 per cent, depending on the movie theater's size and volume of business. For the rest of France the range was 15 to 31 per cent.[29]

In Germany the entertainment tax on cinema admissions was set at a per-ticket rate: 10 per cent on tickets costing up to 3 marks, 15 per cent on tickets of 3 to 5 marks, 20 per cent on those priced between 5 and 10 marks, and 25 per cent on tickets costing over 10 marks.[30] Local tax rates, as in France, however, were much higher. In some cities, such as Bonn and Düsseldorf, they ranged between 60 and 80 per cent.[31] In the first few years of the decade the closing of some movie theaters was occasionally explained as having resulted from "ruinous" local taxes.[32] But while German theater owners sometimes banded together to protest the tax rates, they did not threaten strikes as did their French counterparts.[33] Ironically, perhaps, it was the inflation and monetary crisis that peaked in early 1923, which brought widespread reductions in taxes on cinema admissions. The inflation created trouble in all branches of the film industry, but particularly for movie-theater owners. One trade journal described the situation as the "twilight" of the German cinema.[34] During the worst days of the inflation some 50 Berlin cinemas were forced to close and another 100 or so were rumored to be on the brink of collapse.[35] It had been one thing for municipalities to impose high tax rates on cinema admissions as movie-going boomed in the years just after World War I. It was quite another thing, politically unfeasible, to continue those taxes through the hardships of the inflation. At the height of the inflation Berlin, Munich, Leipzig, and Hamburg all reduced their local entertainment taxes. Scores of smaller cities and towns were quick to follow this example.[36]

The shock of the inflation had turned the tide in favor of the movie-theater owners. In 1926 the German Ministry of Finance recommended that taxes on movie-theater admissions be stabilized in the range from 16.7 to 20 per cent.[37] The proposal was merely advisory. The central government could not impose its will on the municipalities in this matter. Nonetheless, by 1928 the guidelines had been more than fulfilled. By the beginning of that year taxes on cinema admissions in Germany had leveled out at around 15 per cent.[38]

According to a law adopted in 1921, any film judged to be of artistic or national educational ("volksbildernerisch") value could be allowed a reduction of up to 50 per cent of the normal tax on admissions to it.[39] The first feature film to enjoy this advantage was *Fridericus Rex* (directed by Arzen von Czerespy, 1922). In some quarters the film was considered to evoke monarchist sentiments, and a number of cities hence refused to make good on the central government's promise of a tax rebate for it.[40] The incident established a precedent. Throughout the decade municipalities balked repeatedly at granting such rebates.[41] Munich even adopted a city ordinance stating it would pay no attention at all to the "dictates" of the central government in such matters.[42] In retrospect, it is most surprising that the granting of a tax break to certain films met with so little protest from the film industry. A scheme that seemed on the surface to be wide open to abuses and favoritism was evidently carried out in such a manner as to offend very few film-makers.

During the 1920s it was often claimed that the French government was hostile or indifferent to the native film industry. Frequently cited as support for this claim was the government's failure to force a reduction in local taxes on film admissions. By comparison, the German government's policy on most film matters was more constructive. But on the specific issue of taxes, while the system of tax breaks for certain films was positive, the German government really did little directly to reduce them. The lowering of taxes resulted primarily as a response to an almost unprecedented economic crisis. The most important question, however, is what effect higher admissions taxes had on the French cinema. Sometimes the impression is given that the French film industry as a whole labored under undesirable conditions because of high entertainment taxes.[43] In truth, the admissions taxes only directly affected the business prospects of the movie theaters, not the production side of the industry. Any real trouble in the French cinema was in film production. The cinemas themselves, in spite of the high taxes on admissions, flourished. Statistics for the 1920s show that the number of movie theaters per capita in France grew more quickly than in any other industrialized country in the world during the decade.[44]

A survey of the film trade journals for both France and Germany in the 1920s indicates that the issues of limiting foreign-film imports and reducing entertainment taxes occupied much of the film industry's time and energy in both countries. In historical perspective these issues both seem to have paled in importance. The issue of greater significance to this study is the question of censorship of films: how it was conceived and carried out in both France and Germany during the great decade of the silent film.

In France, censorship of plays, music-hall performances, and films had ceased in 1906. During World War I, however, a film censorship service was created by the "Préfecture de Police" in Paris.[45] In July 1919 this "service" was formalized into a national film-censorship board. The board had 30 members. Its chairman was Paul Ginisty, a former theater manager, who held the post throughout the 1920s.[46] The censorship law contained two particularly important articles. One permitted film producers, directors, and scenario writers the right to protest—orally or in writing—negative decisions made by the board. The other established that no decision of the censorship board would take precedence over the right of local police to prohibit the showing of certain films in pursuit of maintaining public order and safety.[47]

For nearly a year and a half the censorship board functioned without banning a single film. Then, in December 1920, the Ministry of the Interior, reacting to protests from Chinese government representatives in Paris, ordered the adventure film *Li-Hang le cruel* recalled from circulation. This occurred although the film had already been cleared by the censorship board. A few cuts were made in the film, and it was rereleased within weeks, playing throughout France in spite of continued complaints by Chinese diplomats.[48] At the same time, possibly in order to cover up the fact that it had yielded to pressure by the Chinese government, the government also recalled the film *L'Homme du large* (directed by Marcel L'Herbier). The Interior Ministry demanded cuts in three scenes. The cuts were made, and the producer, Léon Gaumont, suggested that L'Herbier throw in another cut to assure the government of his good intentions. Within a few weeks of its recall the film was reissued "en bonne et due forme."[49]

The deepest fear of the film industry was that local authorities would abuse their legal rights. In 1921 that fear materialized. The Préfect of the Departement du Var announced that henceforth all films portraying scenes of murder, robbery, assassination, sabotage, or any other "criminal atrocities and outrages" would be banned in the province. Shortly thereafter, the Préfect of Alpes-Maritimes proclaimed that all movies containing depictions of banditry, other criminal activity, or "attacks upon the public morality" were forbidden there. A series of court cases ensued, culminating with the highest court's decision toward the end of 1921 overruling the actions of the Préfects. The judgment was a victory for film-industry interests, albeit an incomplete one. The court upheld the constitutional right of local authorities to ban films already cleared by the national censorship board in instances involving a threat to the public order. The judicial decision only clarified that local authorities could not practice "a priori" censorship as the two Préfects had done.[50] In spite of film-industry misgivings about the limited decision, it evidently served to keep local authorities from being overzealous in using these prerogatives in the future. In 1928 a new law was adopted by the National Assembly stipulating that local police or other officials could ban a film only when a threat to public order and safety was clearly demonstrable.[51]

The French national censorship board was usually generous in its decisions. The judicial process dealt effectively with overzealous local officials and limited their powers in film matters. Nonetheless, many involved in the French cinema hoped for the abolition of censorship of films altogether. When elections in 1924 produced a "left wing" majority in the Chamber of Deputies, rumors spread that this new parliament might end film censorship.[52] Such talk, and the hope that went with it in some quarters, came to naught. The French national censorship board actually became more active after 1924 and reached the peak of its activities in 1926. In that year, having passed 1,264 films, the board banned 51 others.[53] Almost all the films banned in that year, as well as in other years of the 1920s, were forbidden because of their erotic or lewd contents. In this regard the French censorship board relaxed its standards after 1928, the approval of the Czech-made film, *Erotikon*, marking a turning point.[54] The other evil the censorship board monitored was unnecessary brutality in film scenes. Objections to such sequences were usually satisfied by having the film-maker make a few cuts to minimize their impact. At the beginning of 1928 the board announced that any films dealing with World War I in a humorous or comic manner would be banned.[55]

Between 1919 and 1929 only two French-made films were banned on overt political grounds. They were *L'Argent* (an adaptation from an Emile Zola novel, directed by L'Herbier) and *Les Nouveaux monsieurs* (by Jacques Feyder).[56] The former was approved for distribution after some minor changes were made in it; the latter met more difficult opposition. Feyder, with the help of his friend the film director Henry Roussel—who reputedly had good political connections—brought the film before the censorship board for a second time. In spite of Roussel's contact work, the ban on the film, whose plot was considered to insult the French parliament, was upheld. After some soul-searching Feyder then made a single cut, eliminating a scene of a brawl among members of the Chamber of Deputies, and the film was promptly cleared.[57]

In contrast to the practice of letting native films pass the censorship board after a few apt cuts were made, harsh decisions were rendered in the 1920s against German- and Soviet-made movies. After an attempted boycott of all German films right after the war petered out, the French national censorship board adopted a hard line on German films. Ernst Lubitsch's *Madame Du Barry* was banned on the grounds that it was anti-French.[58] G. W. Pabst's *Freudelose Gasse* and Bruno Rahm's *Dirnenträgodie* were both forbidden because they dealt with prostitution. *Asphalt* (directed by Joe May), which portrayed the corruption of a young police officer by a fast woman, was likewise banned in France.[59] The French censors also took exception to Fritz Lang's adventure film about undercover agents, *Spione*.[60] In general, German films were subjected to harsher review, and numerous cuts in them were demanded by French censors. Still, German films were shown in France. The prohibition on Soviet movies was nearly total. In the middle of the decade the French government enforced the prohibition of Sergei Eisenstein's *Battleship Potemkin* in spite of heated public protests against the decision.[61] It became common practice that the censorship board would rule against Soviet films, though a few of them were still shown in violation of the censor's ban in some of the small "art" cinemas of Paris.[62] In 1928 the French Ministry of Public Education and Fine Arts announced formally what had already become standard procedure: All Soviet films, without exception, were to be denied approval by the censorship board.[63]

In Germany film censorship on a national scale had come to an end in November 1918 with the collapse of the Imperial regime. Some elements in the film industry hoped that a proposed article of the new Weimar constitution, guaranteeing freedom of the press and freedom of "expression," would be interpreted so that movies would be free from censorship.[64] The hope seemed naive. A month before the new constitution was ratified, the government had commissioned a study on the feasibility of establishing a film-censorship system.[65]

By spring of 1919 Germany was experiencing waves of protest against a new type of film that had appeared at the end of the war. Called "Aufklärungsfilme," these movies limited themselves to the domain of sexual enlightenment.[66] In June 1919 the film journal *Die Lichtbildbühne* editorialized that if the German film industry were burdened with a censorship law, the guilt for this would lie with the makers of these erotic films, which were being distributed under the guise of contributing to the "scientific" understanding of human sexuality.[67] In August the showing of the film *Die Gelübde der Keuschheit* (*The Vows of Chastity*) in Düsseldorf was protested by the audience, which stormed the stage, tore down the screen, and then rushed into the street to stage a wild, impromptu anti-Semitic demonstration.[68] The film had been produced by the Deutsche Bioscope Company and directed by Nils Chrisander[69]; the anti-Semitism evoked in the riot was evidently a result of the common notion that all the "enlightenment" films were produced by money-hungry Berlin Jews. The incident in Düsseldorf inspired reactions throughout Germany. Bavarian authorities ordered *Gelübde der Keuschheit* (which was considered an insult to Catholicism) closed in Munich, although the film had been playing there without disturbance.[70] The film was also forbidden in Frankfurt am Main.[71] And in Kassel cinema owners soon gave in to pressures from local politicians and "other influential persons," agreeing to show no more "Aufklärungsfilme" in their movie houses.[72]

In the next weeks, the agitation for censorship of films increased noticeably throughout Germany. In the midst of this agitation the *Lichtbildbühne* changed its tune. The journal now argued that the "enlightenment" films were not to be blamed for public demands for censorship, but rather that movies were being made the scapegoat for all the ills of modern society.[73] Pro censorship groups were forming across the Reich.[74] German municipalities were beginning to take censorship matters into their own jurisdictional hands.[75] Thus, the film industry was not displeased when national censorship of movies was established by law in May 1920.[76]

The law established two censorship boards, one sitting in Berlin, the other in Munich. Theoretically, the Munich board was to function for Bavaria, Hesse, Baden, and Württemberg, while the one in Berlin would cover the rest of Germany. In practice, however, approval of a film by either of the boards permitted it to play anywhere in the Reich. And the panels of both boards were appointed by the central government, which annoyed the South German

[53]

states, particularly Bavaria.[77] Article two of the law exempted all newsreels and "landscape films" from the censor's review. Article five established that no child under six years old could enter a movie theater in Germany, and the age limit was raised from six to ten years of age in 1929.[78] The law further stipulated that the board might restrict access to certain films for all persons under 18.[79] Provisions for enforcement and punishment of violations were defined in Germany straight off, as opposed to France where penalties for violating the censorship law were not codified until 1928.[80] Anyone in Germany apprehended showing a lewd film was subject to a one-year imprisonment and a 1,000-mark fine.[81] Permitting youths to see films prohibited to them also carried stiff penalties.[82]

Throughout the 1920s the greatest concern of both the public and the government in Germany in regard to film censorship centered around the issue of which films should be forbidden to persons under 18.[83] Religious groups and other organizations repeatedly protested that trashy movies were "ruining" Germany's youth. And in 1921 the Social Democrat party called for tougher censorship standards, particularly in sorting out which films might be seen by young people.[84] By contrast, in France there was little interest or concern in this matter. Persons of any age could go to movie theaters, and a limited youth ban on certain films applied only to persons under 16. In Germany, the banning of certain films to youth was vigorous. Up until 1922 between 70 and 80 percent of all films shown there were forbidden to persons under 18.[85] Later in the decade, as censorship standards in general were relaxed, in an average year 25 to 30 per cent of the films shown in Germany were prohibited to young people.[86] In France during the 1920s only 5 to 8 per cent of the films shown were forbidden for young audiences in each year of the decade.[87]

Throughout the 1920s the governments in two German states—Bavaria and Hesse—repeatedly protested that the

[54]

national film-censorship board's standards were too lax.[88] The central government ignored these complaints, and local authorities only rarely challenged a few films that had already been cleared by the board. Police in Bamberg stopped showings of the film *Glaube und Heimat* in 1922 on the grounds that the movie's plot was offensive to local religious feeling.[89] The film *Fridericus Rex* encountered local opposition in Hesse and Westphalia in the same year. In this instance, the two respective state governments merely asked the censorship board in Berlin to review the film again in hopes of having it banned. The request was categorically denied.[90] The most-renowned banning of a film by local authorities occurred in 1923 in Munich. Early in the year, after Nazis picketed the theater in which *Nathan der Weise* (an adaptation from a Lessing play directed by Manfred Noa) was showing, Munich police banned the film outright. Called on to explain the forbidding of a film that had been approved by the national censorship board,[91] a representative of the Munich Police wrote:

In plain words the content of this film [*Nathan der Weise*] is that the Jew is everything, and all others, be they Christians or Moslems are nothing. The film's development of this theme is carried out with typical Jewish prejudice which is bound to injure the feelings of those who think differently. In these politically tense times this film would cause particular offense, because so large a part of the population sees in the Jews the cause of its unhappiness.[92]

As in France, so also in Germany, film producers, directors, and scenario writers had the right to personally appeal negative decisions of the censorship board. As the film director Karl Grune wrote of one such incident: "Once they [the censors] wanted to forbid my film *Eifersucht*. I went myself to the censors and discussed the matter with them, explaining what the tendencies [sic] were meant to portray. The gentlemen perceived and understood, and the prohibition was not carried through."[93]

Recourse to such appeals before the censorship board were rare. And little wonder, for the banning of films in Germany was rare. Up until 1922, 90 films were banned in Germany as against 5,300 that were approved. Later in the decade the censor became even more liberal:

Year	Films Reviewed	Films Banned
1924	1,174	20
1925	2,748	30
1926	2,768	14
1927	3,173	5
1928	3,483	11
1929	3,327	10

Even in the most active year of film censorship, 1925, the number of films forbidden represented just over 1 per cent of the total number of movies submitted for review.[94]

There was, however, a pattern of political censorship of certain films. The impetus for this came from the German Foreign Ministry. The guidelines for the Ministry's intervention in movie matters were clear: (1) to prevent the showing of German-made films that might offend a particular foreign government, and (2) to ban films that might give a bad impression of the German Republic to foreign regimes. In pursuit of the first of these aims, the Foreign Ministry acted three times during the 1920s. In 1923 the Foreign Ministry persuaded the censorship board to ban *Das Totenmahl auf Schloss Hegalitz*, an adventure film about the Turkish-Serbian war that might have offended the government in Istanbul.[95] Another instance was in 1927 when the movie *Luise von Coburg* (portraying the amorous frolics of the second daughter of King Leopold II) was forbidden so that the Belgian monarchy would not be offended.[96] And in an incident that raised considerable protest in the film industry for a brief time,[97] the feature *Die Flucht aus dem Heere der Heimatslosen*, depicting desertion from the French foreign legion, was banned.[98]

[56]

In pursuit of its second goal the Ministry was more active. In 1922 the Foreign Ministry directed the Ministry of the Interior (under whose supervision the national film censorship board functioned) to pursue henceforth a policy of banning all films produced by groups of war veterans or right-wing political parties. This, it was explained, was necessary to avoid creating the erroneous impression abroad—particularly in France—that Germany was preparing a war of revenge for the defeat of 1918.[99] The films in question were usually short movies of veterans' parades or other similar patriotic demonstrations. Thus, for example, the film of a veterans' parade in memorial to the slain anti-French saboteur, Leo Schlageter, was banned. And in spite of repeated efforts by the state government in Bavaria to have the ban lifted, it held.[100] In 1924 a similar film of a procession held by a veterans' league in Braunschweig was prohibited.[101] In June of the same year, however, the national censorship board approved a veterans' film entitled *Die Moltke-Denkmalsweihe in Halle*. As soon as the Foreign Ministry learned of this, the film was recalled and promptly banned.[102] To add legal weight and international impact to its campaign against such films, the Foreign Ministry lobbied successfully for an amendment to the general film-censorship law. Under a new provision (1929) any German-made film banned by the censor in Germany would also be automatically forbidden for export to a foreign country.[103] The Foreign Ministry skillfully engineered the banning of a film of the 1927 National Socialist Party Convention,[104] as well as the filmic record of the *Ehrentag der deutschen Armee und Marine in Nürnberg*.[105] So determined was the Foreign Ministry in its efforts to keep the extreme political right off the silver screen that the Ministry habitually ordered footage of right-wing political gatherings deleted from newsreels through most of the decade. This was in direct and open contravention of the law of 1920, which granted newsreels full immunity from film censorship.[106] In the same spirit, the feature film *Die schwarze Schmach*—critical of the Allied occupation of the Rhineland—had been banned in 1922 at the Foreign Ministry's bidding.[107]

During the 1920s the German Foreign Ministry did not limit its activities to seeing to it that certain films were banned. After the Rapallo accords of 1922 the Ministry lobbied—often against strong opposition—to see to it that Soviet-made films were cleared by the censorship board for distribution in Germany. The Foreign Ministry's insistence, for example, that Sergei Eisenstein's *Battleship Potemkin* not only be cleared by the censor but also approved for youthful audiences produced sharp protests from the state governments of Bavaria, Württemberg, Thuringia, and the Minister President of Prussia.[107] The Ministry of Defense locked horns with the Foreign Ministry over the matter of permitting Soviet films to be shown in Germany, claiming that not banning such films was "committing suicide," but the Foreign Ministry prevailed.[108] Unable to sway the national censorship board, the army took to posting "controllers" outside movie theaters in which Soviet-made films were playing to prevent soldiers from entering such cinemas.[109] After Alfred Hugenberg took over UFA in 1927, the firm ceased its distribution of any Soviet-made films.[110] Smaller distributors simply picked up the business. Soviet films continued to play in Germany; the Foreign Ministry remained singularly consistent in its support for them. When the national censorship board in Berlin hesitated in approving the Soviet-made film *Black Sunday* (which dealt with the St. Petersburg revolt of 1905), the Foreign Ministry sent a communiqué to the board pointing out that German-Soviet relations were far more important than qualms about the film harbored by any of the board members. The film was swiftly approved for distribution.[111] One Soviet film, *Storm Over Asia*, even enjoyed the unusual honor of playing German cinemas with the benefit of a government-granted tax reduction.[112]

In both France and Germany during the 1920s the respective film-censorship policies were hardly such as to have been detrimental to the native film industry. Neither country exercised the legal prerogatives of film censorship with enough precision or enough vigor to have had much impact on the contents of native-produced films. Interestingly, insofar as overt political concerns seemed to have played much part in the entire business of film censorship in both France and Germany, issues of foreign, rather than domestic, policy were primarily involved. This is dramatically clear in the sketch of the activities of the German Foreign Ministry that has been presented here. The French government was apparently exercising an extension of its foreign policy, mixed with concern over the possible impact of revolutionary movie themes, in banning Soviet films—extending a kind of celluloid "cordon sanitaire" to the cinema. But in France, too, diplomatic interests seemed to prevail in censorship matters. *Li-Hang, le cruel* was recalled from circulation, after all, to placate an offended foreign government.

The comparative effect of film censorship on the movie business in the two countries is difficult to estimate. The German government forged a policy more stable than its French counterpart with regard to the powers of local authorities in the matter of banning films. Film-makers in Germany should have been comfortable in realizing that a movie approved by the central film-censorship board could play the whole country with little effective local opposition. In France this was more of a question mark throughout the decade. But the greatest potential commercial impact on the movie business through censorship must have been through the instrumentality of designating certain films as being forbidden to youthful audiences. In this regard, the policies of the German censors provided the basis for far greater potential losses in revenue to film-makers than was the case in France. Adolescents between the ages of 12 and 18 provided a sizable portion of the potential audience for almost any film distributed nationally, and the exclusion of this group from so many films in Germany must have been the most important financial function of film censorship in either France or Germany during the 1920s.

Since films have become generally popular, almost all societies in which they are shown have developed some system of censorship or control over them. Some would say that this reflects an ongoing elitism that permeates governmental cirlces and the most influential and articulate strata of society. The evidence for this would seem to be that historically movies have been subjected to much more rigorous scrutiny and control than books, legitimate theaters, the other performing arts, and entertainments in most countries. Others would argue that this merely shows an understanding of the unusual directness and power of the motion picture rather than betraying a snobbism aimed at the movies because they are "mass" entertainment. Whatever the case, the history of censorship indicates that controls have been directed primarily toward protecting audiences from eroticism and excessive violence and brutality in films. Since access to movie theaters has usually been comparatively cheap and easy, most countries have adopted special protections for youth, usually in the form of a more or less elaborate rating system. The censorship of films in both France and Germany during the 1920s was, in general, in keeping with this general pattern. Censorship decisions seem in most cases to adapt themselves to general changes in attitude in society. There is no evidence that the relatively few films that were banned in both France and Germany during the period were not, indeed, films whose contents would have been offensive to a segment of the population. Behind the scenes in moviemaking there is always self-censorship. Since the advent of the feature film, big movies are an expensive business. Producers will usually be cautious. In trying to appeal to a broad, mass, national audience, the avoidance of overtly controversial material or of contents that might offend too many in the potential audience for a given film prevails. More important than the censorship policy may be the film producer's sense of what will sell and what will not. The erotic "enlightenment" films that appeared in a very troubled Germany right at the end of World War I were already fading from the scene when the censorship law of 1920 dealt them a death blow. In a way, it was a mercy killing. They had outlived their relatively short period of scandalous popularity quite quickly. In the long run, the film will be, in an age of mass audience interest in the cinema, a conservative medium of expression. There will be few new ideas and few direct challenges to the basic assumptions of a society in its feature films. Criticism of society will be peripheral and marginal if it is to be found in the contents of popular films at all. On behalf of society's self-interest in the perpetuation of its own system and its own premises, the market place may serve as a better control on the content of films than any censorship board ever could.

N O T E S

1. Howard Lewis, The Motion Picutre Industry (New York: 1933), p. 221. The cost of adding foreign titles to an average-length feature film during the silent era was often less than $500.00.
2. L'Action française (Paris), 5 October 1922, p. 2.
3. Alexander Jason, Jahrbuch der Filmindustrie (Berlin: 1923), I, p. 37.
4. Bonsoir (Paris), 24 January 1924, p. 4.
5. Cinéma-Spectacles, no. 457, 26 February–3 March 1928, p. 8.
6. L'Ami du peuple (Paris), 5 May 1928, p.5.
7. René Jeanne and Charles Ford, Histoire encycolpédique du cinéma (Paris: 1947), I, p. 205.
8. Lewis, op. cit., pp. 404, 405.
9 .André Chevanne, L'Industrie du cinéma (Bordeaux: 1933), pp. 111, 112; also, Lewis, op. cit., p. 417.
10. Charles Ford, Cinéma et mass media (Paris: 1969), p. 66.
11. Ergebnis der Besprechung über Film Ein-und Ausfuhr am 23. Januar 1920 im Reichsministerium, Folio 1–298, R 431/2497, pp. 241–3, Bundesarchiv Koblenz.

12. H. H. Wollenberg, *Fifty Years of German Film* (London: 1948), p. 14.
13. *Der Film-Kurier*, 3. Jahrg., no. 71, 24 March 1921, p. 1.
14. Communiqué from the Reichswirtschaftminister to the Unterstaatssekretär in der Reichskanzlei, 10 January 1922, Folio 1—298, R 431/2497, pp. 203, 304, Bundesarchiv Koblenz.
15. *Der Film-Kurier* took the lead among German film trade journals in denouncing editorially proposals to impose limits on the importation of foreign films. Various issues of the journal, for the years 1920 and 1921 especially, offer rich insights into the tone and tenor of such arguments.
16. Lewis, *op. cit.*, pp. 399, 400.
17. Siegfried Kracauer, *From Caligari to Hitler* (Princeton: 1947), p. 133. The most thorough treatment of the German "contingent" system and its abuses is found in Fritz Olimpsky, *Tendenzen der Filmwirtschaft und deren Auswirkung auf die Filmpresse*, unpublished dissertation, Friedrich Wilhelm Universität, Berlin, 1931, pp. 43–55.
18. UFA Records, Package R 109, Section 121, copy of the contract between UFA and Famous-Players-Lasky Corporation and Metro-Goldwyn-Mayer, dated 31 December 1925, indicate a disregard for the German contingent law as pertaining to the importation of foreign films. Bundesarchiv Koblenz.
19. *Le Courrier cinématographique*, 18ème année, no. 7, 12 February 1927, p. 12.
20. *Ibid.*, no. 5, 29 January 1927, p. 20.
21. Paul Leglise, *Histoire de la politique du cinéma francais*: "Le Cinema et la IIIème republique" (Paris: 1970, pp. 54, 55. See also V. Guillaume-Danvers, "Parlémentarisme et cinéma," *La Cinématographie francaise*, no. 55, 22 November 1919, p. 14.
22. Paul de la Borie, "Le Cinéma proteste et revendique," *La Cinématographie française*, no. 116, 22 January 1921, pp. 4, 9, 10.
23. *L'Action française* (Paris), 10 November 1922, p. 2.
24. *Bonsoir* (Paris), 17 January 1922, p. 3.
25. *Ibid.*, 4 January 1923, p. 3; Also, Auguste Nardy, "La Question des taxes cinématographique," *Bonsoir* (Paris), 24 January 1923, p. 3.
26. Leglise, *op. cit.*, p. 56.
27. *Le Courrier cinématographique*, 19ème année, no. 25, 21 June 1924, p. 6.
28. *Der Film-Kurier*, 6. Jahrg., no. 156, 4 July 1924, p. 3.
29. Lewis, *op. cit.*, p. 412.
30. *Der Kinematograph*, 16. Jahrg., no. 190, 9 April 1922, p. 3.
31. Jason, *op. cit.*, p. 39.
32. *Der Kinematograph*, 17. Jahrg., no. 840, 25 March 1923, p. 16; *ibid.*, nos. 863/864, 2 September 1933, p. 8.
33. *Die Lichtbildbühne*, 12. Jahrg., no. 2, 11 January 1919, p. 36.
34. *Der Kinematograph*, 17. Jahrg., no. 850, 3 June 1923, p. 5.
35. *Der Film-Kurier*, 6. Jahrg., no. 31, 5 February 1924, p. 1. See also

Peter Bächlin, *Der Film als Ware* (Basel; 1947). In *The Sociology of Film Art* (London and New York: 1965), George Huaco maintains (p. 51) that the inflation in Germany in 1923 "favored the film industry, for the rapid currency depreciation that destroyed savings and the rationale for savings stimulated spending keeping movie theaters filled." The evidence from the 1920s indicates that the opposite was true—movie-going declined.

36. Heinz Udo Brachvogel, "Steuerprobleme von gestern und heute," *Der Kinematograph*, 18. Jahrg., no. 920, 5 October 1924, pp. 31, 32. Also, *Der Kinematograph*, 17. Jahrg., nos. 867/868, 7 October 1923, p. 9, and *Der Film-Kurier*, 6. Jahrg., no. 18, 21 January 1924, p. 1; *ibid.*, no. 29, 2 February 1924, p. 1; *ibid.*, no. 43, 19 February 1924, p. 1.

37. Communiqué from Der Reichsminister der Finanzen to die Herren Mitglieder der Reichsausschusse II, IV, und VII, 3 June 1926, Folio 1–287, R 431/2498, pp. 263–8, Bundesarchiv Koblenz.

38. Friedrich Zgliniki, *Der Weg des deutschen Films* (Frankfurt a.M.: 1955), p. 309.

39. *Der Kinematograph*, 16. Jahrg., no. 792, 23 April 1922, no page number.

40. Hans Traub, *Die UFA* (Berlin: 1943), pamphlet, no page number.

41. For example, Flensburg refused to honor a promised tax reduction for Fritz Lang's *Nibelungs; Der Film-Kurier*, 6. Jahrg., no. 124, 26 May 1924, p. 1. Munich rejected a tax rebate for F. W. Murnau's *Der letzte Mann; Der Kinematograph*, 19. Jahrg., no. 941, 1 March 1925, p. 35. Other instances like these were common throughout Germany.

42. *Der Kinematograph*, 19. Jahrg., no. 938, 8 February 1925, p. 15.

43. Lewis, *op. cit.*, p. 406.

44. *Der Film-Kurier*, 3. Jahrg., no. 21, 25 January 1921, p. 1. Also, Chevanne, *op. cit.*, pp. 84, 85; Georges Sadoul, *Le Cinéma devient un art* (Paris: 1952), II, p. 421.

45. G.-Michel Coissac, *Histoire du cinématographe* (Paris: 1925), p. 435.

46. *Ibid.*, pp. 435, 436.

47. *La Cinématographie francaise*, no. 40, 9 August 1919, p. 9; *Die Lichtbildbühne*, 12. Jahrg., no. 34, 23 August 1919, pp. 24, 25.

48. *Le Courrier cinématographique*, 10ème année no. 52, 25 December 1920, p. 39. See also Leglise, *op. cit.*, p. 64.

49. Leglise, *op. cit.*, p. 65.

50. *Ibid.*, pp. 65, 66.

51. *Ibid.*, pp. 69, 70. See also *La Cinématographie francaise*, no. 489, 17 March 1928, p. 3. Oddly, the French censorship law did not stipulate penalties for violations of it. In 1928 such violations were decreed to be subject to a fine of one to five hundred francs each.

52. *Der Film-Kurier*, 6. Jahrg., no. 142, 18 June 1924, p. 2.

53. *Le Courrier cinématographique*, 18ème année, no. 5, 29 January 1927, p. 20.

54. Leglise, *op. cit.*, p. 66.

55. *Cinéma-Spectacles*, no. 452, 22–28 January 1928, p. 4.
56. Leglise, *op. cit.*, pp. 66, 67.
57. *Bulletin Internationale de cinématographie*, 2ème année, no. 3., March 1931, pp. 35, 36.
58. Leglise, *op. cit.*, p. 67. *Madame Du Barry* was banned in other countries on different grounds. Austria forbade the film out of fear that it would promote "revolutionary sentiments"; see *Die Lichtbildbühne*, 13. Jahrg., no. 4, 24 January 1920, p. 24. And Hungary objected to presumed "Bolshevist" tendencies of the film: *Der Film-Kurier*, 3. Jahrg., no. 53, 3 March 1921, p. 1.
59. Leglise, *op. cit.*, p. 67.
60. *Le Courrier cinématographique*, 19ème année, no. 23, 9 June 1928, p. 20.
61. Leglise, *op. cit.*, pp. 66, 67.
62. *La Cinématographie francaise*, 9ème année, no. 438, 26 March 1927, pp. 25, 26. See also Bryher, *Film Problems of Soviet Russia* (Territet: 1929), pp. 134 ff.
63. Jean Lenauer, "Censorship in France," *Close-Up*, vol. IV, no. 5, February 1929, p. 53.
64. Oscar Kalbus, *Vom Werden deutscher Filmkunst* (Altona-Bahrenfeld: 1935), I, p. 41.
65. Report of the Reichsfilmstelle to the Unterstaatssekretär in der Reichskanzlei, 26 July 1919, Folio 1–298, R 431/2497, pp. 32, 33, Bundesarchiv Koblenz.
66. Otto Kriegk, *Der deutsche Film im Spiegel der UFA* (Berlin: 1943), p. 81.
67. *Die Lichtbildbühne*, 12. Jahrg., no. 25, 21 June 1919, p. 11. The article emphasized that the most prominent producer/director of these erotic films was Richard Oswald, a Jew, and suggested that the making of these films was a particularly Jewish enterprise.
68. *Die Lichtbildbühne*, 12. Jahrg., no. 32, 9 August 1919, p. 20. A thorough and detailed description of the riot is found in a letter from the Rheinische Lichtbild-Aktien-Gesellschaft to Reichskanzler Bauer, 14 August 1919, Folio 1—298, R 431/2497, pp. 41, 42, Bundesarchiv Koblenz.
69. Gerhard Lamprecht, *Deutsche Stummfilme 1919* (Berlin: 1968), p. 54.
70. *Der Film*, 4. Jahrg., no. 33, 16 August 1919, pp. 22, 23.
71. *Deutsche Lichtspiel Zeitung*, 8. Jahrg., no. 22, 29 May 1920, p. 5.
72. *Die Lichtbildbühne*, 12. Jahrg., no. 33, 16 August 1919, p. 21.
73. *Ibid.*, no. 34, 23 August 1919, pp. 25, 26.
74. *Ibid.*, no. 46, 15 November 1919, p. 21. See also an article by a proponent of tougher film-censorship legislation: E. Krebs, "Die Reichs-Lichtspielzensur," *Deutsches Volkblatt* (Stuttgart), 25 June 1921, p. 1. Also, *Der Kinematograph*, 13. Jahrg., no. 674, 3 December 1919, no page number.

75. *Die Lichtbildbühne,* 13. Jahrg., no. 10, 6 March 1920, p. 31; *Deutsche Lichtspiel Zeitung,* 8. Jahrg., no. 24, 12 June 1920, pp..5, 6; *Der Film-Kurier,* 2. Jahrg., no. 116, 3 June 1920, p. 1; Jason, *op. cit.,* I, p. 29.

76. Letter from the Reichministerium des Innern to Herrn Staatssekretär in der Reichskanzlei, 19 June 1920, Folio 1–298, R 431/2497, pp. 281, 282, Bundesarchiv Koblenz.

77. Communiqué from Der Reichsminister des Innern to alle oberste Reichsbehörden und die nachgeordneten Behörden, 6 July 1920, Folio 1–298, R 431/2497, p. 293, Bundesarchiv Koblenz. Until 1920 film affairs were under the aegis of the Foreign Ministry; in that year they were transferred to the care of the Minister of the Interior.

78. Communiqué from Der Reichsminister des Innern to Herrn Reichssaekretär in der Reichskanzlei, 4 February 1929, Folio 1—269, R 431/2499, pp. 174—80, Bundesarchiv Koblenz.

79. A copy of the Ausfuhrungsverordnung zum Lichtspielgesetz vom 12. Mai 1920, Folio 1–298, R 431/2497, pp. 283–5, Bundesarchiv Koblenz.

80. See note number 51.

81. Albert Hellwig, "Unzüchtige Filme und Filmzensur," *Der Film-Kurier,* 3. Jahrg., no. 223, 24 September 1921, p. 5.

82. *Der Film-Kurier,* 6. Jahrg., no. 50, 27 February 1924, p. 1.

83. Letter, Namens der in den Feldauer Bischofkonferenzen vereinigten Oberhirten deutscher Diözesen to the Reichsminister des Innern, 20 April 1923, Folio 1–287, R 431/2498, pp. 106, 107, Bundesarchiv Koblenz. Also, a letter from Zentrumsabgeordneter Dr. Hompel to Reichskanzler Marx, 22 January 1924, Folio 1–287, R 431/2498, p. 134, Bundesarchiv Koblenz.

84. *Der Film-Kurier,* 3. Jahrg., no. 204, 1 September 1921, p. 1.

85. *Die Reichsfilmprüfung* (Berlin: 1922), pp. 55–205. This pamphlet, printed by the press of the *Lichtbildbühne* magazine, listed all decisions of the central film censorship board of Berlin for the years 1920–22.

86. Alexander Jason, *Jahrbuch der Filmindustrie* (Berlin: 1933), IV, p. 47.

87. *Le Courrier cinématographique,* 18ème année, no. 5, 29 February 1927, p. 20.

88. *Der Kinematograph,* 16. Jahrg., no. 790, 9 April 1922, p. 1. Also, letter from the Zentralstelle zur Förderung und Jugendpflege in Hessen to the Hessisches Ministerium des Innern, 5 February 1924, Folio 1–1287, R 431/2498, p. 137, Bundesarchiv Koblenz.

89. *Allgemeine Kino-Börse,* XII. Jahrg., no. 3, 21 January 1922, p. 43.

90. Jason, *Jahrbuch der Filmindustrie,* I, p. 39.

91. *Die Lichtbildbühne,* 16. Jahrg., no. 9, 3 March 1923, p. 23; *ibid.,* no. 1, 6 January 1923, p. 21. See also Jason, *Jahrbuch der Filmindustrie,* I, p. 48.

92. *Die Lichtbildbühne*, 16. Jahrg., no. 4, 27 January 1923, p. 16.

93. A. Krasna-Krauz, "A Letter on Censorship," *Close-Up*, vol. IV, no. 2, February 1929, p. 58.

94. Alexander Jason, *Handbuch der Filmindustrie* (Berlin: 1932), IV, p. 47.

95. *Der Kinematograph*, 17. Jahrg., no. 872, 4 November 1923, p. 3.

96. Letter from the Deutsche Gesandschaft, Brussel to das Auswärtige Amt, 8 October 1927, Folio 1—269, R 431/2499, pp. 40, 41, Bundesarchiv Koblenz.

97. *Die Lichtbildbühne*, 14 Jahrg., no. 25, 18 June 1921, pp. 25, 26.

98 *Der Film-Kurier*, 3. Jahrg., no. 139, 16 June 1921, p. 1: *Vossische Zeitung* (Berlin), 3 October 1926, p. 7, and two separate letters, one from the Vertretung der Reichsregierung, München to the Reichskanzlei, 6 August 1926, Folio 1—287, R 431/2498, p. 271, and the other from the Preussischer Ministerpräsident to the Reichskanzler, 19 May 1926, Folio 1—287, R 431/2498, p. 260, both in the Bundesarchiv Koblenz.

99. Communiqué from the Reichsminister des Innern to sämtliche Landesregierungen, und, in Preussen, das Ministerium des Innern, 23 September 1922, Folio 1—287, R 431/2498, p. 70, Bundesarchiv Koblenz.

100. Letter from the Reichskanzler to den Vertreter der Reichsregierung in München, Herrn Gesandten Haniel von Haimhausen, 7 August 1923, Folio 1—287, R 431/2498, pp. 117—9, Bundesarchiv Koblenz. Also, a letter from the Vertretung der Reichsregierung in München to das auswärtige Amt durch die Reichskanzlei, 27 August 1925, Folio 1—287, R 431/2498, p. 209, Bundesarchiv Koblenz.

101. Jason, *Jahrbuch der Filmindustrie*, II, p. 490.

102. *Der Film-Kurier*, 6. Jahrg., no. 144, 20 June 1924, p. 2.

103. Letter from the Reichsminister des Innern to the Reichssekreatär in der Reichskanzlei, 4 February 1929, Folio 1–269, R 431/2499, pp. 174–80, Bundesarchiv Koblenz.

104. Letter from the Vertretung der Reichsregierung München to das auswärtige Amt, 3 December 1927, Folio 1—269, R 431/2499, pp. 45—7, Bundesarchiv Koblenz.

105. Letter from the Vertretung der Reichsregierung München to das auswärtige Amt, not dated, Folio 1—287, R 431/2498, pp. 277, 278, Bundesarchiv Koblenz.

106. *Der Film-Kurier*, 6. Jahrg., no. 144, 20 June 1924, p. 2; *ibid.*, no. 234, 3 October 1924, p. 3.

107. Letter from the Reichsminister des Innern to Herrn Grafen Zech, Vertreter der Reichsregierung in München, 22 May 1922, Folio 1—287, R 431/2498, pp. 61—3, Bundesarchiv Koblenz.

108. Letter from the Reichswehrminister to the Reichsminister des Innern, 7 April 1927, Folio 1–267, R 431/2499, p. 17, Bundesarchiv Koblenz.

109. Letter from the Wehrkreiskommando I (1. Division) to the Reichsministerium, 16 March 1927, Folio 1—269, R 431/2499, p. 18, Bundesarchiv Koblenz. These activities of the army "controllers" in Germany were also reported in the French film trade journal, *Le Courrier cinématographique*, 19ème année, no. 29, 21 July 1928, p. 7.
110. Klaus-Dieter Bärthel, *Die Rolle der Universum Film A.G. bei der ideologischen Beeinflussung der Massen im Sinne der reaktionärsten Kräfte des deutschen Monopolkapitals und ihrer agressiven Pläne, 1918 bis 1933*, unpublished dissertation, Karl Marx Universität, Leipzig, 1965, pp. 46, 47.
111. Letter from Sachverständiger des auswärtigen Amtes to the Sachverständiger bei der Oberfilmprüfstelle in Berlin, not dated, Folio 1—269, R 431/2499, p. 19, Bundesarchiv Koblenz.
112. Lenauer, *op. cit.*, p. 53.

The Film
as National
Folklore

In 1919 the young French film director Jean Renoir said of his career: "I am beginning to understand how one should work. I know that I am French, and that I should work in a way that is *absolutely national*."[1] Renoir's sentiments reflected a mentality that was shared not only by most of his fellow film-makers in France but by their counterparts in Germany as well. The 1920s were *the* epoch of the national film. During that decade the most successful of commercial film directors in France—Jacques Baroncelli, Louis Feuillade, and Henri Diamant-Berger, for example—all expressed themselves in favor of national, French cinema.[2] The directors who associated their work with a style in film-making called "impressionism," Marcel L'Herbier, Germaine Dulac, Abel Gance, and Jean Epstein, agreed with the movement's chief theoretician, Louis Delluc, that their films should be thoroughly French in style and spirit. The impressionist slogan demanded: "French cinema should be cinema, and French cinema should be French."[3]

Throughout the 1920s the daily press and the film-industry trade journals defended, elaborated, and promoted the notion that native-produced films should incorporate themes and motifs worthy of contemporary French culture and appropriate to it.[4] The most articulate of the French writers on cinema as art, Ricardo Canudo and Maurice de Waleffe, received little attention from those actually working in the film industry except for the undue notice given to their arguments that the French cinema should be first and foremost national in its content and character. Canudo's proposal that each film should contribute to the "national folklore" drew interest and praise in particular.[5] Producers competed throughout the decade to be associated with "the most French of films,"[6] and movie-theater owners vied for customers by advertising the "most truly French" programs.[7]

The most successful French films of the 1920s were assumed to be those that expressed the essence of the "national mentality." Conversely, films that failed at the box office—or, more generally, difficulties of the film industry at large—were blamed on a national inability to comprehend the spirit of the cinema and cinematography. The Minister of Public Education and Fine Arts in France at the beginning of the 1920s, André François-Poncet, was fond of explaining any misfortune suffered by the French film industry by claiming: "The latin spirit is ill-adapted to the cinema."[8] Variations on this theme were numerous. The film critic Jean Lenauer liked to conclude that native-produced films that failed did so because the French were too "attached to the word" and were thus incapable of responding to visual images.[9] Another theoretician, René Schwob, argued that the problem was not that the French were too attached to the "word," but that they were obsessed with painting and architecture, which dissipated the national talent and inclination for either music or the cinema. The only peoples capable of creating great cinema, he maintained, were the Americans, because they were "infantile," and the Russians, because they were "mystical."[10] Yet another explanation for some films being unsuccessful was offered by Jacques Sichier, who wrote that the main problem was that the French mentality was unsuited to comprehending a true sense of the "epic."[11]

Repeatedly during the 1920s the German trade journal *Der Film-Kurier* claimed that French film producers and directors made films of a too decidedly French character.[12] By 1924 the journal was so distressed with what it had seen of French productions that it commented that almost every French film had as its "raison d'être" the portrayal "of what God had achieved through the French as His agent."[13] It was ironic that *Der Film-Kurier* embarked on this particular editorial campaign, for the journal employed the most eager of celebrants of the virtues of the "national, German film," Heinz Michaelis. His special contribution to the widespread notion of film as folklore was the proposition that each movie must in its own unique way be an apt national reflection of "the spirit of the times."[14]

Michaelis did not have to argue his case at great length in the Germany of the 1920s, though he made his living doing just that. Most of the people involved in the production of Germany's major films left little doubt that they favored the notion of national cinema. The production chiefs at UFA were committed to a policy whereby even films that were, to some extent, intended to favorably impress foreign audiences were to do so on the basis of their being genuinely and uniquely Germanic.[15] Franz Osten, a production manager at Emelka Film, Germany's second largest production firm, went on record in support of national film:

> ... everyday life is in a very unique way folkish—it is in every nation somewhat different, and is thus related to the individu-

ality of the people, its mores, and its historical development and culture. *Nation* is the ultimate goal of a shared destiny: a community of thought, action, and feeling . . . It is precisely from this point of view that we are correct in speaking of a *German* film. But this has meaning in another sense as well—in regard to the genre, that is, to the species of the film itself.[16]

Richard Ott, the general director of the film firm Deulig, also claimed that he thought of each German film as a unique expression of the "Volk".[17] In 1921 a representative of the Foreign Ministry urged native film-makers at every level of production to see to it that every feature film, no matter what its dramatic content, created a "picture of German character" ("ein Bild deutschen Wesens").[18] The editor in chief of the *Reichsfilmblatt* editorialized that each German film should preserve in itself "a nationalism in the best sense of the word."[19] And even the most prominent German film director to hold leftist political views, G. W. Pabst, proclaimed himself to be fully in support of the concept of national cinema.[20]

For the producer Karl Melzer the issue was primarily commercial: "The national characteristics of film are not an obstacle, but rather a promise of business success."[21] "The German film should be German" was a battle cry for those who thought of film as merchandise just as it was for those who thought of film as art. Successful German films were rightly referred to as "national products."[22] For by the beginning of the 1920s it was generally agreed that talk of "international films" was pipe dreaming. According to the film historian Georges Sadoul, the handful of international coproductions made during the 1920s shared one characteristic: "sterility."[23] Moreover, they all shared the same commercial fate: failure at the box office.[24] It was the "national" film to which audiences responded most favorably. And as the British film critic Iris Barry, who was often quoted in Germany, put it: "The internationality of films is possible only on a national basis."[25]

The export of films and their appeal to foreign audiences raised complicated questions during the 1920s. People in the movie business agreed that mass audiences around the world sometimes enjoyed seeing "the representation of foreign customs" on the silver screen, and that this opportunity "to be transported to a foreign world" was the basic appeal of foreign films.[26] Still, only a limited number of films out of any nation's total production were considered exportable, and of that group of films some were considered appropriate for one foreign audience but not for another. As the general manager of the American firm Fox Films said during a visit to Berlin in 1920: "Only a portion of the films which we produce comes into consideration for the German audience, since the others are not in keeping with the German taste."[27] Four years later a study of movie-going habits in Germany concluded that foreign films in general "simply could not satisfy the needs of the public." Even American productions, which were usually the most popular foreign films with German audiences, were sometimes too much aimed at the American mentality ("zu sehr auf die amerikanische Psyche eingestellt").[28] In the United States, film distributors found that only a handful of German-made films annually were suitable for general distribution.[29] The same held for French films. The general director of Gaumont visited the United States in 1923 and reported back to Paris that American audiences were often as not bored with French films, just as French audiences frequently became bored with American movies.[30] In turn, French films were almost never shown in Germany, for they were believed generally unsuitable there, and British films were practically unknown in Germany.[31]

In 1922 when a German film that had been very successful at home failed abysmally in England, Die Lichtbildbühne commented that such commercial catastrophes would not occur if distributors had a better understanding of "national psychology."[32] Yet throughout the decade accurate assumptions about national tastes in films were difficult to make. One of the most popular German films of the decade, *Die Nibelungen* (directed by Fritz Lang, 1924), was distributed worldwide and failed at the box-office everywhere abroad.[33] A similar fate befell the French production of *Napoléon* (directed by Abel Gance, 1927). The film had filled movie houses in the cities and provinces of France, yet reaction to it in the United States, for example, was downright hostile. One American movie-theater owner wrote: "Doubtless a great subject, and is probably considered a great production somewhere, but we can't see it." And another reflected on his experiences with *Napoléon:* "The worst bunch of junk I have run in four years. . . . I screened it in two towns and even the children couldn't stand it."[34] Such experiences were frequent, and often it was discovered that a film could be distributed successfully in a foreign country only after extensive editing had produced a fundamentally new version of it.[35]

Still, the 1920s experienced a vigorous international trade in films, which must be understood in the commercial context of the times. Some smaller and less-developed countries had practically no native film industry, and these were naturally inundated with foreign films. Moreover, once a feature film had had its run of a few months to half a year in its native land, there was literally nothing better to do with it than ship it abroad. A film that no longer had commercial value at home was just as well fitted with foreign titles and distributed in a foreign market. This situation created the "dumping" of films on foreign markets even though it was well understood that there was little chance of their achieving widespread popularity. A polling of German movie-theater owners for the years 1925 through 1930, for example, revealed that the popularity of foreign films with German audiences was extremely low despite the frequency with which foreign films played on movie-theater bills throughout the Reich.[36] In general, insofar as foreign movies were successful at the box office, their popularity was always skewed toward audiences in large cities. The main audience for foreign films in all countries during the 1920s was an urban, cosmopolitan audience, which differed in character from the broad, mass, national audience to which the most popular native-produced movies appealed. Certainly some foreign films were box-office hits. Some Hollywood films, for example, those of Charlie Chaplin and Jackie Coogan and many silent Westerns, were very popular in France. But Chaplin was not particularly popular in Germany; German taste for American films generally ran to the grandiose epics.

The success of some foreign films does not, however, invalidate a study of the most popular native-produced films as dreamlike reflections of the shared latent concerns of the mass audience in a given country. For, fundamentally, the basic maxim to be drawn from looking at the issue of foreign films and their appeal or lack of it is this:

> As we know, not every film can be exported into just any country in the world.... It is very important to realize that if on the one hand images of any film are based on natural human propensities, they are on the other hand influenced by unique collective and individual experiences.... It is therein that we have a demonstration establishing the transformation of collective images from one country to another, from one human community to the next.[37]

The rhetoric of "national" cinema that was common in both France and Germany during the 1920s reflected the economic realities of the movie business in both countries. The competitive nature of that business in both France and Germany meant that everyone involved in commercial feature film production "had to slave to make something which was popular."[38] To be popular meant to appeal to the mass, national audience. To do this meant to develop standardized, national types of films; hence the advent of one genre of film in a particular country that found no counterpart in another. But even more important than the differences found between one national cinema and another are the subtle nuances of imagery and the oblique repetition of theme and motif that may not be evident in viewing these movies casually. The function of these subtle differences is to create the real stuff out of which a national cinema is made and to serve to define that cinema's relationship to its society. "In only the most rare instances does a film reflect a societal reality; rather, certain ideals, aspirations, and ideological conceptions—in other words, specific dispositions which exist within the society—create a *psychological* reality which because of the misleading effects of realistic photography can resemble a social reality."[39]

Film communicates by the elaboration of precise, symbolic visual material that creates both a mood and a story. The result is a medium whose primary appeal is psychological. And the psychology of the most popular movies must be collective. For while it is quite reasonable to assume that a particular film—or a particular sequence within a film—may appeal on the basis of individual psychological tendencies, it hardly follows that a cluster of popular, national films would appeal to millions on the same basis. The symbolism of a popular movie must be such as to create the basis of a shared, collective psychological appeal to at least a portion of the mass audience. When a group of popular films is analyzed as a dreamlike reflection of a group psychological reality, the following statement by the sociologist I. C. Jarvie takes on its full meaning: "Apart from anthropological field work, I know of nothing comparable from a point of view of getting under the skin of another society as viewing films made for the home market."[40]

One film theorist has written: "And the great majority of people go to the movies simply for the sake of going to the movies. For them, the cinema is an end in itself."[41] This study takes exception to that notion. In the 1920s, when the cinema was as popular as it was, there were surely some persons who went to any movie indiscriminately, out of habit. Yet, the history of film as merchandise in every country in every period indicates that such individuals do not account for a large portion of the mass audience for films. There are a lot of digits between a box-office flop and a smash hit, which is the primary reason for studying only the most popular films of France and Germany as a reflection of society in the period 1919–29.[42] There is a difference between a broadly popular film and one produced in the same country at the same time that fails to appeal to the mass audience. And that difference, which may be assumed to be a function of a given film's relationship to society, is one key to understanding the social significance of particular films in their historical context.

In the preceding chapters a sketch of some of the pertinent aspects of the movie business in both France and Germany during the 1920s has been provided. It serves to make several things clear. The film industries in both countries were relatively competitive. Censorship in both countries during the era had little or no overt, measurable impact on film content, and governmental interference in the actual production of films was nil. The audience for the most popular films was broad; without regard to class, sex, age, or urban/rural differences, the most popular films in both countries were made as "national products" that would appeal to the broadest spectrum of the national audience as a whole. Still, there are those who will wonder whether public preference truly expressed itself in determining which films actually became most popular. This suspicion raises, specifically, the question of what role advertising, publicity, and film criticism played in influencing the popularity of movies in France and Germany during the 1920s.

In the daily press in both countries advertisement of movie-theater programs was normally limited to simple announcements of which films were playing at what times. Display advertising was rare.[43] More energy and money were expended on trade advertisements placed in journals to interest movie-theater owners in renting specific films.[44] Grand publicity campaigns on behalf of a film were unusual, though not unknown. UFA's effort to publicize *Das Kabinett des Doktor Caligaris* (directed by Robert Wiene, 1919) drew attention at the time, and historians of the cinema have often cited the incident. Posters flooded Berlin, some proclaiming, "You must become Caligari!" Others, less challenging, read "You must see Caligari!" or "Have you seen Caligari?"[45] This poster campaign was apparently limited to the German capital, and *Caligari*'s business at the box office nationwide was not exceptionally good. The French equivalent of the *Caligari* promotion was the publicity prepared for *Le Secret de Rosette Lambert* (directed by Raymond Bernard, 1920). The distributor provided 150,000 post cards announcing the film, which movie-theater owners then mailed to prospective viewers.[46] In 1920 a new form of movie promotion was introduced in the United States: the showing of "trailers" (later commonly known as "coming attractions"), featuring highlights from films billed for future presentation at a given cinema.[47] Before the year was out, "trailers" were in use in Europe, too.[48] Whether the practice of projecting these film clips became as widespread in Europe during the 1920s as it did in the United States is difficult to determine. But "trailers" evidently were the main form of promotion for most films in France and Germany during the 1920s. At all other levels, however, European film advertising was decidedly inferior to the publicity efforts of producers, distributors, and movie-theater owners in the United States.[49] In Europe film publicity was usually handled by the distributor, not by the production company.[50] Average expenditures for such publicity were strikingly low.[51] Reputedly, film publicity improved in both France and Germany during the second half of the decade. According to a contemporary article on the subject, a simple principle had prevailed until then: to get "the cheapest and most colorful poster."[52] During the 1920s the most effective film publicity was considered to be the brochure which each film-goer received when attending a movie theater. It resembled a playbill, provided a cryptic summary of the film in question, and presumably might be passed on to friends, relatives, and acquaintances.[53] If there was any direct correlation between film publicity and film popularity in France and Germany, it was not established in the 1920s, nor can it be established in retrospect. Many films that were ostensibly well advertised were flops. Many that were felt to be poorly advertised became box-office hits.[54]

It was much the same with film criticism. In contrast to theatrical criticism, which exerted considerable influence on the success or failure of a stage play, movie criticism played no such role.[55] The cinema was a new medium. Traditional standards of dramatic criticism were inappropriate to it, and new standards of evaluation were slow to evolve. The composition of the movie audience was completely different from that of the theatrical audience. While the literate, articulate, and well-educated did go to films in France and Germany during the 1920s, the mass audience for movies was also composed of many people who were not in the habit of reading criticism of any kind. Film criticism—as the word is normally understood—was limited to major dailies in the largest cities. Newspapers in smaller cities and towns limited comments on films playing at local movie theaters to brief plot summaries devoid of judgment or analysis. What film criticism there was exerted no measurable influence on which films actually became box-office successes.[56] In Germany as early as 1919

Die Lichtbildbühne noted the box-office failure of numerous films that had been "glowingly critiqued."[57] In both France and Germany throughout the 1920s this pattern held: There was no direct correlation between favorable criticism and a film's popularity.[58]

Undeniably, there are a number of variables—publicity and criticism included—that might have had something to do with the popularity of certain films. The importance of these factors was, however, minor. The so-called "star system," for example, was basically a Hollywood gimmick designed to standardize production in a large country in which national taste was exceptionally difficult to identify. This device did not really take hold in Europe during the 1920s. Some French and German actors and actresses were popular and enjoyed a certain following. But the presence of a given actor or actress in a particular film could not assure a movie's box-office success. In the 1920s typecasting was the order of the day in Europe. It was the "type" of role an actor or actress successfully interpreted repeatedly that was at the core of his or her popularity. The "type" was a product of a genre or kind of film that had become popular at a particular time. The function of the leading actor or actress was, hence, quite different from that of the Hollywood "star." Yet even Hollywood's experience with the system indicates that the appeal of a "star" is limited. Miscasting or the performance of a screen player in a flop has often meant the abrupt end of a career in movies. In a number of instances, the mass audience has lost its taste for a "star" for no easily discernible reason. During the 1920s the mass, national audience selected its most popular films primarily on the basis of their plots. The plots of the most popular films of the decade—some 48 for France and 63 for Germany—are the basis for the analysis and interpretation of what those films meant to the native audiences in both countries, respectively.

NOTES

1. Georges Sadoul, "À la recherche de quelques fils conducteurs."*Le Point,* 12ème année, LIX, 1962, p. 7.
2. André Lang, *Déplacements et villégiatures littéraires* (Paris: no date), p. 148. *Anthologie du cinema* (Paris: 1967), II, p. 251; unpublished interview with Henri Diamant-Berger, April 1971.
3. Georges Sadoul, *Histoire du cinéma français* (Paris: 1962), pp. 24, 25.
4. For example, see Auguste Nardy, "Vindicta," *Bonsoir* (Paris), 3 July 1923, p. 3, or the issue of *L'Action française* (Paris), 22 September 1922, p. 2, for typical articles on "national" cinema. Also, a number of articles by V. Guillaume-Danvers in *La Cinématographie française,* no. 12, 25 January 1919, pp. 29, 30; *ibid.,* no. 15, 15 February 1919, pp. 15, 16; *ibid.,* no. 55, 22 November 1919, pp. 16 and 25.
5. No author, "Zur Frage des nationalen Films," *Der Film-Kurier,* 6. Jahrg., no. 103, 1 May 1924, p. 1.
6. *Le Courrier cinématographique,* 18ème année, no. 21, 21 May 1927, p. 7.
7. *Ibid.,* 14ème année, no. 29, 19 July 1924, p. 14 and *ibid.,* no. 30, 26 July 1924, entire edition.
8. Carl Vincent, *Histoire de l'art cinématographique* (Brussels: no date), p. 4.
9. Jean Lenauer, "La Situation du cinéma français," *Close-Up,* vol. IV, no. 5, May 1929, p. 65.
10. Henri Fescourt *et al.,* *Le Cinéma: des origines à nos jours* (Paris: 1932), p. 231.
11. Jacques Sichier, "Dans le cinéma français l'aventure ne depasse pas le coin de la rue," *L'Écran,* January 1958, p. 10.
12. Paul Ickes, "Offener Brief an Henry Roussel, Paris," *Der Film-Kurier,* 3. Jahrg., no. 174, 28 July 1921, p. 3. See also no author, "Das französische Kinopublikum," *Der Film-Kurier,* 6. Jahrg., no. 153, 1 July 1924, p. 1.
13. *Der Film-Kurier,* 6. Jahrg., no. 67, 18 March 1924, p. 1.
14. Heinz Michaelis, "Der Weg des deutschen Films," *Der Film-Kurier,* 6. Jahrg., no. 1, 1 January 1924, p. 11. Also, Heinz Michaelis, "Ein deutscher Gesellschaftsfilm," *Der Film-Kurier,* 6. Jahrg., no. 9, 10 January 1924, p. 1; Heinz Michaelis, "Der Zeitgeist im Film," *Der Film-Kurier,* 6. Jahrg., no. 136, 11 June 1924, p. 1.
15. Lotte Eisner, Fritz Lang's biographer, revealed to me that Lang had told her that he was as obsessed with the idea of national Germanic film as was his wife at the time, Thea von Harbou, a scenario writer— for that matter, everyone else in German film was of the same mind.
16. Franz Osten, "Der deutsche Film," *Allgemeine Kino-Börse,* XI. Jahrg., no. 13, 20 March 1921, p. 219.

17. Richard Ott, "Plus oder Minus," *Der Film-Kurier*, 6. Jahrg., no. 1, 1 January 1924, p. 27.
18. Hans Mahraht,"Propaganda im Film," *Der Film-Kurier*, 3. Jahrg., no. 72, 26 March 1921, p. 1. Mahraht was director of division IX of the German Foreign Ministry.
19. *MKB Film-Rundschau* (Essen), 3 July 1928, no page number.
20. K. MacPherson, "Die Liebe der Jeanne Ney," *Close-Up*, vol II, no. 6, December 1927, pp. 18, 19.
21. Charles Ford, *Bréviaire du cinéma* (Paris: 1945), p. 89.
22. No author, "Die nationale Grundlage des Films," *Der Film-Kurier*, 6. Jahrg., no. 65, 15 March 1924, p. 9.
23. Georges Sadoul, *Histoire du cinéma français*, p. 46.
24. René Jeanne and Charles Ford, *Histoire encyclopédique du cinéma* (Paris: 1947), p. 46.
25. No author, "Das Märchen von der Internationalität des Films," *Der Film-Kurier*, 3. Jahrg., no. 110, 12 May 1921, pp. 1, 2; no author, "Die nationale Grundlage des Films," *Der Film-Kurier*, 6. Jahrg., no. 65, 15 March 1924, p. 9.
26. Elie Faure, "The Art of Cineplastics," in Daniel Talbot, *Film: an Anthology* (Berkeley: 1967), pp. 8, 9. See also *Der Film-Kurier*, 6. Jahrg., no. 87, 10 April 1924, p. 1.
27. *Die Lichtbildbühne*, 13. Jahrg., no. 15, 3 April 1920, p. 21.
28. *Der Film-Kurier*, 6. Jahrg., no. 139, 14 June 1924, p. 1.
29. Lothar Stark, "Richtlinien für neue Exportmöglichkeiten," *Der Film-Kurier*, 3. Jahrg., 13 August 1921, p. 3.
30. Auguste Nardy, "Le Public américain devant l'écran," *Bonsoir* (Paris), 24 July 1923, p. 3.
31. Willy Haas, "Haben wir einen internationalen Überblick?" *Der Film-Kurier*, 6. Jahrg., no. 8, 9 January 1924, p. 1.
32. *Die Lichtbildbühne*, 15. Jahrg., no. 4, 21 January 1922, p. 35.
33. No author, "Die Nibelungen durchgefallen," *Der Film-Kurier*, 6. Jahrg., no. 225, 23 September 1924, pp. 3, 4.
34. Kevin Brownlow, *The Parade's Gone By* (London: 1969), p. 563.
35. Bryher. "The War from the Angles," *Close-Up*, vol. II, no. 1, July 1927, pp. 16–18.
36. *Der Film-Kurier*, 12. Jahrg., no. 129, 1 June 1930, p. 2.
37. Mario Ponzo, "Le Cinéma et les images collectives," *Revue Internationale de Filmologie*, Tome II, no. 6, no date, pp. 150, 151.
38. Ricardo Canudo, *L'Usine aux images* (Geneva: 1927), p. 11. See also J. Sternheim, "Was will das Publikum im Film sehen?" *Der Film-Kurier*, 3. Jahrg., no. 159, 11 July 1921, p. 1; *La Cinématographie française*, no. 83, 5 June 1920, pp. 27–30.
39. Paul Heimann, "Der Film als Ausdruck der Gegenwartskultur," *Universitas*, 12. Jahrg., no. 4, 1957, p. 352. For some comments to the same point, see J. P. Mayer, *Sociology of Film* (London: 1948), p. 275.
40. I. C. Jarvie, *Towards a Sociology of Cinema* (London: 1970), p. 4.
41. André Boll, *Le Cinéma et son histoire* (Paris: 1941), p. 105.

42. One of the major difficulties with Siegfried Kracauer's *From Caligari to Hitler* (Princeton: 1947) is that the psychological tendencies of the German nation as a collectivity are discerned to exist primarily in films that were mainly "cult items" and hardly popular films at all. Kracauer set out to analyze the repetition of popular myths in the films but became bogged down in studying the images of the art films of the Weimar period for the most part. The emphasis on popularity as an index of a given film's importance in its relationship to society is a major way in which this study differs in approach from Kracauer's.

43. This conclusion is based on a survey of daily newspapers for the period, including *Le Populaire* (Paris), *Bonsoir* (Paris), *Figaro* (Paris), *Le Matin* (Paris), and *L'Action française* (Paris). For Germany, the *Berliner Tagesblatt* and the *Berliner Morgenpost* were the newspapers checked in detail for each year from 1919–29. For both France and Germany, numerous other newspapers for smaller cities were scanned.

44. Repeated examples to support this point are found in all of the film trade journals for both France and Germany, cited elsewhere in the notes for this, and other, chapters.

45. George Huaco, *The Sociology of Film Art* (New York and London: 1965), p. 34.

46. *La Cinématographie française*, no. 107, 20 November 1920, p. 89; *Le Courrier cinématographique*, 18ème année, no. 27, 2 July 1927, p. 13. Also, Lucien Wahl, "Films de guerre français," *La Revue du cinéma*, 3ème année, no. 22, 1 May 1931, p. 21.

47. Howard Lewis, *The Motion Picture Industry* (New York: 1933), p. 242.

48. *Le Courrier cinématographique*, 10ème année, no. 6, 7 February 1920, p. 6.

49. *Der Film-Kurier*, 2. Jahrg., no. 96, 9 May 1920, pp. 1, 2. Similarly, *Die Lichtbildbühne*, 16. Jahrg., no. 20, 19 May 1923, p. 38; *Der Kinematograph*, 17. Jahrg., no. 830, 14 January 1923, p. 13.

50. Lewis, *op. cit.*, pp. 230–32.

51. Friedrich Zgliniki, *Der Weg des deutschen Films* (Frankfurt a.M.: 1955), p. 435.

52. G. Velloni, "Les belles façades du cinéma," *Le Courrier cinématographique*, 14ème année, no. 19, 10 May 1924, p. 5. Also, no author, "Moderne Filmplakate," *Der Kinematograph*, 17. Jahrg., no. 864, 9 September 1923, pp. 7, 8; Curt Wesse, "Die Filmpropaganda im Jahre 1923," *Der Film-Kurier*, 6. Jahrg., no. 1, 1 January 1924, p. 11.

53. See the *Courrier cinématographique*, 10ème année, no. 12, 10 January 1920, pp. 26–35; *ibid.*, 14ème année, no. 7, 16 February 1924, the entire edition. The movie-theater brochures are to be found preserved in the collections of the Bibliotheque Idhec (Paris), the Cinémathèque française (Paris), the Stiftung Deutsche Kinemathek (Berlin), the Staatliches Filmarchiv der DDR (Berlin, DDR), and the Deutsches Institut für Filmkunde (Wiesbaden/Biberich), among other places. They

were so common that many individuals and families still have sizable collections of them.

54. *Die Lichtbildbühne*, 14. Jahrg., no. 17, 23 April 1921, no page number.
55. *Der Film*, 4 Jahrg., no. 20, 17 May 1919, pp. 3, 4, 36.
56. A comparison of the titles of films that can be documented as having been most popular in Germany bears no relationship to their having been well received by critics or not. This can be crosschecked against issues of a periodical called *Film und Presse*, published throughout the 1920s, which printed excerpts from contemporary film criticism drawn from newspapers in the entire Reich.
57. *Die Lichtbildbühne*, 12. Jahrg., no. 4, 25 January 1919, p. 107.
58. Numerous references bear out this contention. Among them are: *Film Echo*, no. 13, 19 December 1921, p. 2; *Deutsche Lichtspiel Zeitung*, 8. Jahrg., no. 38, 18 September 1920, pp. 2, 3; *Die Lichtbildbühne*, 15. Jahrg., no. 2, 7 January 1922, p. 51; *Reichsfilmblatt*, no. 17, 28 April 1923, pp. 1 and 12; Canudo, op. cit., p. 16; Léon Moussinac, *Panoramique du cinéma* (Paris: 1955), p. 55.

The Popular Cinema
as Reflection of
the Group Process
in France, 1919–29

Latent collective meanings of films reveal themselves through analysis of surface film contents. On the conscious level movie-goers are primarily interested in the film story and its cinedramatic development.[1] For the interpretation of a group of films, the cinematographic devices through which content is portrayed are of secondary importance. In some instances, however, the repetition or stylization of certain such devices and techniques in the popular films of a nation may reveal important psychological tendencies. Moreover, the ways in which technical means are used to intensify the impact of certain scenes cannot simply be ignored and in some cases can be of great consequence.

For clarity it is best to begin the process of analysis with the thematic material which is easiest to recognize. Half of the most popular French films of the 1920s handle, in one way or another, an orphan story. The first popular orphan film of the post-World War I era was *Le petit café*, which premiered in early 1919. In the film, orphan Albert Loriflan is a waiter who has been tricked into a 20-year contract by the café owner Philibert. Philibert had learned that Albert had inherited millions from a benefactor before poor Albert himself discovered the good news. Albert cannot enjoy his money because he is bound by the contract to pay a high penalty if he quits his job. A happy ending "à la française" finds Albert out of the contract and in the loving arms of Philibert's daughter. During the 1919 cinema season the orphan theme caught on slowly. In *La Nouvelle aurore* Giselle is an orphan who is eventually reunited with her long-lost father, who had been sent to prison unjustly. But Giselle's reunion with her father stands peripheral to much of the film's complicated plot. Equally peripheral to an intricate drama, albeit emotionally poignant, is the subtheme involving the little girl known as "Petit Ange" in *J'Accuse*. Little Angel is presented to the viewer as an orphan, but she turns out to be the daughter of a French woman who was raped by a German soldier during one of the military attacks of 1914. In another popular production of the year 1919, *Travail*, the orphan story is more fully developed. Josine, a working girl, has been left an orphan and must care for her brother Nanet. She becomes the mistress of the brutal Ragu, and her life is miserable. Eventually, however, she marries the idealist Luc, and little Nanet, who is raised in their loving home, grows and marries the daughter of a wealthy factory owner.

The story of Josine and little Nanet comes closest of all the films of 1919 to paralleling what became an almost archetypal orphan motif in popular French movies of the 1920s. The most intense portrayal of the orphan theme was exploited by French film-makers during the years 1921–26 with repeated box-office success. Louis Feuillade's *Les deux gamines*, for example, depicts the adventures of a

double pair of orphans: Ginette and Gaby, Blanche and Re-
née. The viewer follows them down various rocky roads
until all four attain adulthood and happiness. Two successful filmic adaptations from Lamartine by the director Léon
Poirier—*Jocelyn* made in 1922, and *Geneviéve*, which appeared the following year—centered around orphan stories.
The orphan story in each is different, but the emotional
impact is similar. Jocelyn, a simple country curé, is en-
trusted with the care of an orphaned boy during the Terror of
the French Revolution. The boy is, in fact, a girl; a girl with
whom, in all due course, Jocelyn falls in love. In *Geneviéve*,
the goodhearted heroine from whose name the title comes,
promises her dying mother to care for her younger sister
Josette. Here the orphan theme is elaborated twice over.
Josette comes of age and becomes pregnant by a soldier
who falls in battle. Josette abandons her newborn baby.
When the baby is found by authorities, Geneviéve says the
baby is her own. She goes to jail and on her release learns
that Josette has died and the baby has disappeared. A decade passes. One day Josette's son appears during a thun-
derstorm at Geneviéve's humble door. When his true identity is by chance revealed, Geneviéve becomes his protector
and joins the household of his adoptive parents. In *La
Mendiante de Saint-Sulpice* (1924), twin girls are born
during a German bombardment of a French village in the
year 1870. A cousin of their mother has one of them kid-
naped during the confusion of the German attack in which
his own newborn child has perished. The rogue's aim is to
raise the child as his own and someday cash in on an in-
heritance his own child was due to receive. Years later the
twin girls are united not only with each other but also with
their true mother as well. *Enfant des Halles* (also 1924) is a
typical film by the highly successful commercial director
René Le Prince. A street-urchin orphan of the Paris slums
finds a baby girl abandoned in a pile of vegetables at the
main market. The boy, named Berlingot, "adopts" the baby

girl and takes her to live with the poor family that is keeping him. Later, Berlingot himself is adopted by a rich Canadian couple that has lost its two children in an auto accident. In truth, the little girl found in the vegetable pile was their daughter, who had been picked up and abandoned by a vagabond who happened upon the scene of the auto accident. The wealthy Canadians die years later. Berlingot is left an orphan for a second time, but this time he is left a rich one. He happens to meet a young lady, the very girl he had found abandoned as a baby. They fall in love and marry.

The basic structure in such French orphan films can be stated simply. An orphan, abandoned and alone in the world, is taken in by a protector or reunited with his or her parents. In the dénouement the orphan is invariably rewarded with happiness and health, often with wealth, and sometimes with true love and marriage. In each case the story differs, but this variety reduces to uniformity at the psychic level. The popularity of the orphan theme was recognized by Ricardo Canudo. In his *L'Usine aux images* (1927), to characterize the typical popular French cinema of the decade, he chose as representative the film *Taô*. He described this adventure serial, which premiered in 1921:

> It's about an orphan—naturally; beautiful, noble, and rich— naturally; exposed to interesting persecutions and saved, after many a hazardous adventure, by a young man who is poor, herculean, courageous, and generous—naturally; who turns out by accident to be the Duke de Bellisle, with whom she—just as naturally as ever—falls in love.[2]

Whether the film is set in the jungles of Cambodia as in *Taô* or in the Paris of Napoleon III as in Henry Roussel's *Violettes impériales* (1923), the basic theme in both films is revealed on analysis as similar. *Violettes impériales* was one of the commercially most successful French films of the 1920s. Its story revolves around a poor orphan girl named Violetta who is taken under the protective wing of

[87]

the Empress Eugénie. Violetta is appreciative and demonstrates it when she saves the Empress from an assassin's bomb. Violetta takes Eugénie's place in the Imperial carriage for a visit to an orphan's home. Violetta knows the dangers; the carriage is bombed. But she survives, saved from the worst effects of the blast by a blanket of flowers presented to her by the orphan children. Eugénie rewards Violetta's loyalty by elevating her to the ranks of the nobility, whereupon Violetta can marry the nobleman she loves.

The plot of *Violettes impériales* is simple when compared to the intricate photoplay of *Joueur d'échecs* (1926). Nonetheless, the plot of *Joueur* evolves from an orphan story, indeed, a double orphan story. The main characters are Boleslas, the orphaned son of a countess, and Sophie, an orphan girl of unknown, but evidently impoverished, background. Both are taken in and raised by the Baron von Kempelen. Boleslas becomes a hero of the Polish nationalist movement. His life is endangered, and he is saved only by the unselfish sacrifice of the Baron. Not surprisingly, Boleslas and Sophie discover their true love for each other as they mourn the Baron's death. True love likewise awaits the orphan hero of *Paris* (1924). Jean Fleury, orphaned at an early age and hence forced to relinquish his studies and take a factory job, courageously catches a thief trying to steal Professor Roullet's design for a new locomotive. The model engine explodes, the thief is killed, and Jean convalesces at the side of his one and only true love, Aimée, who will soon be Mrs. Fleury. In *Les Misérables* (1925) Jean Valjean promises the dying young mother Fantine that he will care for her illegitimate daughter. This he does, and little orphan Cosette grows to find true love and happiness in her marriage to the lawyer Pontmercy. The orphan theme is developed in another adaptation from literature, *Les Mystères de Paris* (1922), in which a Duke becomes the protector of the orphaned bistro singer Fleur-de-Marie and later discovers that she is his own daughter. Yet another variation on the theme of the orphan gaining love and security is found in *Visages d'enfants* (1923). A little boy has been embittered by the death of his mother. When one day her vision no longer comes to him, he feels hopelessly abandoned. He is about to jump into the raging torrents of a river when his stepmother appears and saves him. In the arms of this woman, from whom he had felt himself estranged, he now discovers true love and happiness.

The frequency of repetition of the orphan story in the most popular French films of the 1920s is in itself striking. No national cinema of any other land at any other time has been so singularly obsessed with this particular thematic material.[3] To interpret the meaning of the orphan films, caution demands consideration of other thematic material in the same set of films that seems related to the orphan motif.

Logic would first turn to the noteworthy presence of chil dren in French films of this decade.[4] The association is clear: An orphan is a child bereaved of his parents. Among films that portray children, which have nothing to do with the orphan theme proper, *Le Secret de Polichinelle* (1923) and *La Valse de l'adieu* (1928) merit mention. *La Terre promise* does have an oblique reference to an orphan boy adopted by a rabbi, but this is not very important in the movie. *L'Homme du large* (1920) portrays the coming of age of a fisherman's son. Abel Gance's serious-minded *J'Accuse* (1919) makes much of scenes of French children playing at war as the real war rages a few kilometers away. Gance employed the juxtaposition of children and soldiers again in his 1927 film *Napoléon*. Jean Renoir's comedy *Tire au flanc* (likewise 1927) reaches its most poignant satirical moment when a group of soldiers on maneuver run amuck amidst an outing of school children. In *Maldone* (1928) the "restless one," who has settled down temporarily to respectable family life, finds his greatest joy in playing with his young son. In *Travail* the idealist Luc Froment becomes aware of the potential for reconciliation of the social classes when he sees the children of workers playing happily with the children of a factory owner. When the sailor-hero of *Le Baiser qui tue* (1928) fears that he has syphilis, his tortured mind conjures up the worst of all visions: He sees himself attacking his baby son. Finally, the hero of *Crainquebille* (1923) is the little newspaper hawker who befriends a lonely, abandoned, and distraught man. Tenderly and lovingly the boy takes Crainquebille home to live with him.

More examples of children in popular French films of the decade could be cited, but they need not be. The pattern is clear. The meaning of it, however, is complex. On the face of it, the portrayal of children in these popular films is not related to the orphan motif in an illuminating manner. What must be considered is not just what all orphans are— parentless children—but rather what orphans are specifically in the French films that depicted them. The point of all these orphan stories is that an individual is abandoned, lost in the world, and up against great odds. The resolution comes when the orphan is recognized for what he or she truly is. Recognition is followed by reward: being reunited with one's parents or proper guardians or else finding the security and happiness of true love.

What is basic to the orphan movies—being abandoned and alone—is paralleled in another genre of the French popular cinema of the 1920s. Movies that portray the individual attaining his or her greatest achievements when alone and abandoned convey, in different form, the same message as the orphan films.

Abel Gance explained why he made *Napoléon* in a single line: "I did the film about Napoleon because he was a paradox in an epoch which itself was a paradox."[5] That may have been Gance's conscious intention and inspiration, but the emotional emphasis in the film is not on elements of paradox. The dramatic high points come at moments in which Napoleon is alone and abandoned and must master a situation through his force of character. Emphasis on the lone individual abandoned is also exploited in the two Joan of Arc films that were popular with French audiences during the 1920s. This is particularly true of Theodore Dreyer's much acclaimed *La Passion et la mort de Jeanne d'Arc* (1927). The film's action is confined almost entirely to a courtroom in which Joan faces her brutish interrogators. The composition is so dependent on close-up and medium shots that Joan is seen almost exclusively isolated in the frame against a neutral background. There are few titles in the movie, but one of those comes at a dramatic moment when Joan can mumble only: "Alone, alone, alone." Joan is taken to be burned at the stake alone, just as she has suffered the abuses of her interrogators alone. Only in the very last scenes of the film do the townsfolk recognize her true human worth and rise in protest against her prosecutors. In *La Merveilleuse Vie de Jeanne d'Arc* (produced in 1929, two years after the Dreyer film) the message is likewise clear that Joan must stand alone to realize her true heroism.

The dramatic high point in *Le Miracle des loups* (1924) is when young Jeanne, the daughter of an advisor to the French King Louis XI, is surrounded by enemy Burgundians as she is on the way to deliver the King's message to his supporters. As the Burgundians close in on her, the miracle from which the film draws its title occurs. Wolves appear from the nearby forests, form a protective ring around Jeanne, and force the Burgundians to retreat in fear. She gets through to the besieged city of Perrone and delivers the message. "Alone and now orphaned," as a descriptive title informs the viewer, Jeanne rises to lead the defense of the town. When the battle is over, she is united with her long-lost lover, Robert Cottereau.

Jean Valjean, the hero of *Les Misérables*, is a loner when

he first leaves prison. He assumes various disguises and performs a number of good works. At the end of the film he gains belated recognition for all that he has done. In *Travail* Luc Froment is abandoned and scorned by the very people he wishes to help through a visionary reordering of society. Finally, however, he wins their approval and appreciation. The hero of the war film *Chignole* (1919) steals a plane against orders and shoots down a German fighter single-handedly. Thus does he win the praise of his officers and the hand of Sophie Bassinet. In another war film, *La Grande épreuve* (made nine years after *Chignole*), the soldier Paul undertakes alone the risky mission of blowing up a supply depot behind German lines. This he achieves, but he returns to the French trenches badly wounded. He recovers, however, in time to celebrate the armistice with his engagement to the lovely Claire.

Several films already mentioned as examples of the orphan-film genre portray beside the orphan character an abandoned, lonely individual whose good works are recognized belatedly, as in *Jocelyn, Geneviève,* and *Les Mystères de Paris. L'Homme du large* is yet another movie that depicts the final triumph of an individual who has been abandoned. It tells of a fisherman's son who falls in with a bad pack. As punishment, his father binds the adolescent in a fishnet and puts him into a little one-man boat, which is set adrift upon the sea. Alone, abandoned, and disowned, the young man is reborn through this experience. In the final scenes of the film he is seen, brave, courageous, and manly, captaining his own small craft at sea. A similar story of an individual who comes upon hardship, runs amuck, finds herself alone and abandoned, and wins recognition and redemption through her suffering is developed in Jacques Baroncelli's *La Légende de Soeur Béatrix* (1923). In an earlier film by the same director, *Le Secret du "Lone Star"* (1920), the heroine is left alone after her father's suicide. In turn, her fiancé abandons her when she is accused of a felony. In the end she demonstrates her true human worth, whence her innocence is recognized, and she is reunited with her lover.

Most of the popular French films that portray orphan stories or the tales of other abandoned individuals are "hero movies." Interestingly, common components of these films resemble elements discovered by Otto Rank in his studies of myths from various cultures. Rank concluded that "the normal relations of the hero to his father and his mother regularly appear impaired in all these myths."[6] In general, the same is true of the films under discussion. Rank adds: "Summarizing the essentials of the hero myth we find the descent from noble parents, the exposure in a river and in a box, and the raising by lowly parents; followed in the future evolution of the story by the hero's return to his first parents."[7] The characteristic elements of the popular French films of the 1920s are close enough to the characteristics established by Rank for traditional myths to permit of the generalization that in many instances these movies resemble closely the classical and primitive mode of telling a hero story.

In the French popular films the abandonment of an orphan or another hero figure is never literally in a river or in a box. But certain motifs in the films do mesh with these elements, most dramatically the repetition of water imagery and seascapes on the one hand and the significance of landscape cinematography on the other. Seascapes are important in such films as *La Bataille* (1923), *Le Baiser qui tue* (1928), *Coeur fidèle* (1923), *J'Accuse* (1919), and *La Nouvelle aurore* (1919). Water plays a dramatic-symbolic role in *Les deux gamines* (1920) as well. The orphans Ginette and Gaby go to the seashore to spread flowers on the water in memory of their mother, who was lost in a shipwreck. They are offered a ride to the coast by Monsieur Bersange and his sister; this marks the beginning of the process whereby the girls are reunited with their mother, who did not perish in a shipwreck after all. As has been mentioned earlier, the little boy in *Visages d'enfants* is saved from drowning himself in a river, and the young man in *L'Homme du large* is reborn when cast off to sea in a small boat. In *Napoléon* the symbolic birth of the hero occurs when Bonaparte decides to leave behind the comfortable life that could have been his on Corsica and sets out alone in a little boat (using the French tricolor as a sail) upon the seas in search of a greater destiny. Water imagery is also visually important in *Rose France* (1919), *Maldone*, and *Le Secret du "Lone Star."*

This frequent repetition of water imagery is the unconscious representation of group psychic wishes connected to birth. This interpretation follows the established analytical view that water dreams are most often birth related in individual cases.[8] Other material, both manifest and latent, in the French popular films of the 1920s reinforces this interpretation. Landscape cinematography was prominent in these films. And on the surface the landscape passages in the French cinema often seemed incidental and gratuitous: lingering visualizations of countryside with little apparent aesthetic or dramatic justification. In films as different in plot and technique as *La Valse de l'adieu* (1928), *La Femme nue* (1926), *La Dame de Monsereau* (1923), *Un Chapeau de paille d'Italie* (1927), *Taô*, and *Les deux gamines*, landscape cinematography is significant. In the war films *J'Accuse*, *La grande épreuve*, and *Verdun, visions d'histoire* (1927) the elaborate and extensive use of landscape footage is noticeable. Marcel L'Herbier's *Rose France* and *L'Homme du large* both develop a landscape cinematography that is dramatically and emotionally important. The same is true of the single film by Jean Epstein, which achieved broad popularity, *Coeur fidèle*. For the 1920s Jean Gremillion's *Maldone* has frequently been cited in histories of the movies as a masterwork of landscape cinematography.[9] The earliest French feature films in which nature and landscape imagery were fully developed were those directed by Jacques Baroncelli and Léon Poirier,[10] who between themselves were responsible for five of the most popular native-produced films in France during the 1920s.

The most important French "school" of cinematography during the decade following World War I was the impressionist movement. In terms of the social function of film it is not so important that a handful of directors tried to develop impressionism in the film by emphasizing a particular approach to landscape cinematography. More revealing is that many of the devices and techniques pioneered by the impressionists crept into the work of commercial filmmakers. This indicates that the French mass, national audience had a sharper and more sympathetic eye for landscape cinematography than was true of most national audiences.[11]

Though production capital was often hard to come by in France during the twenties, French film producers were remarkably willing to spend money for films shot on location.[12] This preference for shooting on location and filming outdoors (rather than in a studio) would not have been sustained had the results not been appealing to French audiences. Moreover, investment capital in film research in France during the 1920s was earmarked almost entirely for the development of techniques for making color film, while in other countries research time and money was channeled into perfecting a process for producing synchronized sound films.[13] Of the few studios built in France during the decade, most were located in the sunny south near Nice and were constructed as "glass cages" to create a filming atmosphere in which "natural, outdoor" lighting prevailed.[14] The cinema capitalists put their money where they think the audience's heart is. Thus, such investments (in filming on location, the attempt to develop color film, and the building of studios designed to permit natural

[95]

lighting) are significant as part of the psychohistory of a national cinema.

The common visual effect of landscape cinematography in the French films of the 1920s is a sense of affirmation, an impression of being at one with the world. There is no opposition between man and nature in these French movies. Just the opposite is true of German popular films of the same decade. Many of the popular French films of the 1920s allude to the life-giving and sustaining force of nature. As the director Marco de Gastyn described his characterization of Joan of Arc in *La Merveilleuse vie de Jeanne d'Arc*: A peasant, she clings to the soil with all her atavism, as if she herself were a product of that soil."[15] In *La Force de sa vie* (1920) young Jean Paoli returns from Paris to his native Corsica to commune with nature and regain both his spiritual and physical energies. The hero of *Le Baiser qui tue* goes to his native Brittany, where his closeness to the soil speeds his recovery from wounds suffered when he saved his fellow sailors from a shipboard explosion. Napoleon, too, is portrayed as a son of the soil in the Abel Gance film of 1927; Bonaparte's most profound thoughts come to him as he meditates in isolation in the Corsican countryside. Frederic Chopin in *La Valse de l'adieu* returns to the peaceful Polish village of his birth from Paris when he reaches the limits of his emotional energies. The dramatic high point in the grandiose war film *Verdun, visions d'histoire* comes when an elderly farmer shouts to weary French soldiers: "Don't let them pass, comrades." Those words spark the successful French defense against the final German assault. A title explains the farmer's words and their impact upon the troops: "It was as if the land itself were speaking to them."

In general, landscape scenes in the French films of the twenties are developed with a studied patience. The controlled slowness induces the feeling of lingering in the spot being photographed. Landscape footage is frequently edited into the filmic action. The final effect is that the scenes of countryside and nature convey a sense of comfort and affirmation on the one hand and a distinct feeling of "déjà vu" on the other. The editing in French films of the 1920s was slow paced, an observation confirmed by various contemporary comments. Rex Ingram, an American director who sometimes worked in France during the decade, characterized French productions by saying: "The immobility of the entire structural form combines with the amiable inaction of the performers."[16] Considering the most popular French films of the decade, this generalization holds true for almost every one.[17] Elie Fauré devoted much attention in his critical writings on cinema to the slow pace of the editing and the relative lack of visual movement within each sequence in the typical French films of the era.[18] The French style sometimes disturbed foreign viewers in particular. In an open letter published in *Le Courrier cinématographique* in 1928, R. Waage, the director of the "Filmkuset" in Bergen, Norway, claimed that French films were usually received unfavorably by Norwegian audiences because they had "too slow movements."[19] In France itself, however, the reaction to "la lenteur du développement" was most often favorable.[20]

It is in the landscape and seascape passages in French movies that the repetiousness and slowness of the cinematographic development is most emphatic. These settings, and the manner in which they are presented on the screen, combine to create a feeling of comfort, affirmation, and familiarity. It is in just this way that landscape cinematography in the French popular films of the 1920s is akin to water imagery in these same films. The landscape passages represent an unconscious birth motif. According to Freud, individual dreams of landscapes or other localities yield "a convinced feeling of having been there once before," whence landscapes symbolize the mother's womb. This meaning holds for female as well as male dreamers. Freud's original phrase "das Genitale der Mutter" refers in this context to the genital rather than the sexual quality of the mother's equipment.[21] The landscapes in French films represent birth, as do the seascapes. At the symbolic level what seem to be opposites (landscapes/seascapes) are interchangeable, an equivalence affirmed by the distinctive mode of cinematographic presentation in both cases: the camera lingering familiarly and intimately.

The first collective obsession that can be established for the French popular cinema of the 1920s concerns children and birth. The meaning of this obsession can be best understood in light of the demographic stiuation that existed in France after World War I. France was the single major European nation in which the birth rate had leveled off before the end of the nineteenth century. By the 1920s, France's population growth rate had been at a near standstill for almost five decades. In 1890 Arsène Dumont's *Dépopulation et civilisation* had appeared in France,[22] and on the eve of World War I Jacques Bertillon had published *La Dépopulation de la France*.[23] Before 1914 France was not yet losing population; compared to other European nations, however, she was no longer growing. Between 1871 and 1911 the total population growth rate was barely 9 per cent. In the same period population growth in European Russia stood at 53 per cent, in Germany at 57.8 per cent, and in the United Kingdom at nearly 43 per cent.[24] World War I brought France's relatively low population growth rate to a standstill. During the war France lost proportionately the most of any nation in human as well as in material terms[25]; 1,400,000 Frenchmen died, and twice that many were seriously wounded. In crude mathematical terms, the incorporation of Alsace and Lorraine into the French Republic after the war had just about replaced the number of men that had fallen.[26] But, in fact, 30 per cent of all French males between the ages of 18 and 27 had died in the war. This minimized the number of potential fathers in the demographic curve during the decade following the war. The war years themselves were marked by a startling decline in the rate of marriage, a trend that held throughout the 1920s.[27] The fertility rate had fallen during the war years, too, and that decrease was not appreciably reversed in the postwar era.[28] In 1911 France had a population of 41,476,000. In 1921 the population was barely over 39 million. Only by 1936 did France again reach the 41 million mark.[29]

In itself, a standstill in the birth rate and even a slight loss in total population is no cause for undue national concern. Yet just such concern spread in France. At the end of the 1920s Ludovic Nadeau's popular *La France se regarde; Le problème de la natalité* appeared in print. Nadeau concluded that France's claim to being a major power was at stake in the population issue. He backed this argument with specific examples, citing as most important his claim that Germany would be forced to pay its reparations debts only if France began producing progeny at record rates.[30] Another example of concern over France's birth and population growth rate was found in a series of articles printed by the Parisian daily *Bonsoir* in 1923. The items were demographic figures for a French and German town, which were usually printed without further comment, for the message was clear. For example[31]:

Montelimar (France) pop. 13,150		Limarteberg (Germany) pp. 13,400
1	marriages	30
0	births	40
4	deaths	4

The public concern over birth and population in France during the 1920s sprang, to be sure, from fear over France's possible loss of great power status. More importantly, however, that fear was refined by the more immediate concern over a future challenge from the recently defeated, but still larger and stronger, neighbor on the other side of the Rhine. By the early 1920s Germany already counted over 60 million inhabitants, and her rate of population growth was not retarded as was France's. The birth imagery and portrayal of children in the most popular films represent the working off of this pressing group obsession. The wish fulfillment that recurs time and again in these movies is one in which births abound and happy children romp and play with an unconscious eye on the national future. These popular films disguised what they were really about: the psychosymbolic solution of one of the major problems to which postwar France was a sorry heir.

That very problem, however, would have been alleviated had developments in international relations gone as the French were led to believe they would go by the Versailles Conference of 1919. Those 20 million more Germans would have been a minor worry rather than a major threat had the two prime codesigners of the Versailles settlement, the United States and Great Britain, shown themselves willing to live up to guarantees of France's security in the 1920s. This was not the case. Within a year of their formulation, those guarantees were rendered worthless. The collective-security provisions of the Versailles Treaty (Article 16 of the League of Nations charter associated with the treaty, to be exact) were overshadowed by the refusal of the United States to join the League and by England's adoption of an increasingly generous position toward Germany during the 1920s.[32] Wilson and Lloyd George had promised other separate protective treaties to France as well. But those treaties had to be ratified by *both* the United States and England before going into force. The British ratified theirs, which did not take effect, however, as the United States failed to follow suit. Increasingly France became alarmed for her security. She sought then to ensure it by forging a system of Eastern alliances, a project that had begun during the first quarrels with Wilson and Lloyd George even before the Versailles Treaty had been finalized.[33]

The "entente cordiale," under whose aegis France and England entered the war as allies in 1914, became the "rupture cordiale" of the 1920s. France certainly wanted it to be otherwise. Her attempts to go it alone against Germany (notably the 1923 occupation of the Ruhr) as well as her searching out of substitute allies (Poland and the "Little Entente," and collective security through the instrumentality of the League of Nations) were, in retrospect, but a sad charade. What France wanted was a return to the situation in which her security would be guaranteed by her old allies, primarily England and secondarily the United States.

France had been abandoned. She was a diplomatic orphan. This is the primary group psychological meaning of the orphan theme in French movies of the decade following World War I. The orphan films represent a recurrent, dreamlike working off of the French national trauma of having experienced in short order the disintegration of those very alliances that had meant victory instead of defeat in the First World War and that were assumed to be the necessary guarantee of French security for the future. Like the orphans and other heroes of her popular movies, France found herself during the 1920s abandoned, for all practical purposes alone in the world, and up against big odds.[34] The message in those films is almost always the same: The orphan is recognized for what he or she is and is reunited to those who love him or her most, be it parents (i.e., the rightful guardians) or a true love (i.e., the proper partner). On the mass, public level the unconscious wish fulfillment of these films is that France should be recognized for what she truly is, whereupon she would be reunited (i.e., re-allied) to her old protectors England and the United States. There seems to have been two forms to that national wish: Regain the *protectors* of 1917/18, England and the United States; recover the *alliance* with England. The first is represented by the orphan regaining his or her parents, the second, by the regaining of the old, true loved one.

The unconscious group wish in the orphan films finds a

[101]

direct parallel in the number of French films of the 1920s that end in marriage or at least in a partnership that is presumed to be right and lasting. In the discussion of the orphan films, many titles have been cited that end in marriage or engagement. To be added to the list are *Les Exploits de Mandrin* (1924), *La Dame de Monsereau* (1923), *Le Miracle des Loups* (1924), *La Force de sa vie* (1920), *Les Transatlantiques* (1927), *Le Baiser qui tue* (1928), and *Verdun, visions d'histoire* (1927). This in itself is significant, for a word for marriage in French is "alliance," the same word used for a formal diplomatic partnership, an alliance between nations. The association here is clear; it makes the argument all the more compelling that a meaning of these films is the expression of the group psychic wish to see the old protective partnership between France and England formally re-established. The argument is compelling twice over when a common dramatic situation in these popular French films is taken into account as well. Often the marriage or engagement that occurs signifies the re-establishment of a long-standing true love that had in some way, often through a misunderstanding, been interrupted.

In *La Femme nue* (1926), for example, the painter Rouchard falls in love with and marries the model Lolette. Their life together is joy on earth until Rouchard makes the acquaintance of a seductive princess. A misunderstanding occurs between him and Lolette over this. In the end, however, the couple is reunited, and a mutual friend of theirs assures Rouchard: "Fool . . . she has always loved you." In *Violettes impériales* (1923) Violetta cannot return the love of a dashing nobleman because of her impoverished past. Her courageous deeds, however, merit her elevation to the nobility, whence she can be united forever to her lover. In *La Rue de la Paix* (1927) the lovely Manon and her true love, the designer Laurent, have a misunderstanding over her relationship to the millionaire Ally. In the last scenes of the movie Manon and Laurent are happily reunited, and Ally recognizes that these two people truly belong together. The heroine of *La Terre promise* (1924), the Jewess Lia, loves the Christian André. She is urged to sacrifice for the good of all the Jews of her Bessarabian town, however, and marry her wealthy uncle. She is about to do just that when Uncle Moïse himself recognizes that he was mistaken in asking for her hand. Lia and André wed, and the happy couple enters the "promised land" of marital bliss. In *La grande épreuve* (1928) the brave French soldier Paul falls in love with a nurse named Claire. Because of a letter he finds in the pocket of his dying brother Max at the front, he is misled into thinking that he and Max love the same girl. The misunderstanding is corrected. As bells toll the armistice of November 1918, Paul and Claire announce their engagement. The misunderstanding in *Le Secret de Polichinelle* (1923) is on the part of the parents of wealthy Henri de Jouvenal. They disapprove of his marrying the working-class girl Marie. Only when they come to know and love the illegitimate son of Henri and Marie do the elder Jouvenals recognize their error and bless the marriage. In *L'Homme du large* the sister of the young man who has gone bad gives up her lover and enters a nunnery to atone for the brother's sins. As soon as she realizes that her brother has overcome his misspent past, she leaves the cloister and rushes straight to the passionate embrace of her lover. At the end of *Taô*, the Cambodian girl Soun retires to a Buddhist convent. This might seem to be a direct contradiction of what happens in *L'Homme du large*, but it is not. Soun has decided to devote the rest of her life to prayer and meditation, having realized that Jacques, whom she loves, rightfully belongs to his lover Raymonde, to whom he is now united until death do them part.

The common theme shared by all these films can be summarized succinctly. The original love relationship has been interrupted by a misunderstanding. That misunderstanding is recognized for what it really is, whence the correct, original relationship can be re-established.[35] At the group psychic level this means that the original, informal partnership with Great Britain that had collapsed after 1919 because of a misunderstanding (or so the group mind wanted to interpret it) should be recognized as a right and natural partnership. From this would follow the fulfilled wish of the partnership being re-established in a permanent, formal "alliance."

It is noteworthy that when popular French films of the 1920s deal with a romantic triangle, the second (or substitute) partner is portrayed as neither undesirable nor as an enemy. The substitute has come between two lovers only because an unfortunate misunderstanding has separated them temporarily. The substitute lover is simply "less desirable" than the proper partner. The portrayal of the substitute partner is furthermore usually sympathetic in that he or she recognizes the greater force of the true love relationship in the long run and withdraws from the triangle. This elaboration of the triangle story points to the complex diplomatic relationship in which France found herself during the 1920s. When France's original protective alliances dissolved, she turned to a substitute partnership with several Eastern European nations. Based on the so-called "Little Entente," this arrangement was always considered, if not always openly recognized, as a substitute arrangement, a "système hybride, force provisoire."[36] The French really wished that this alternative would give way to the re-establishment of the original partnership. In these films there is, however, an unconscious refusal to offend the substitute partner; thus, the "less desirable" rather than the "undesirable" formulation in the triangle story.

It is common for feature films to portray violent deaths, accidents, murders, crimes, and so forth. Violence as a manifest element in a given cinema reveals little. Of greater importance are the differences from one nation's cinema to another between the ways in which violence occurs and what its meaning is within a particular film. If there are crimes, who is the villain and who is the victim? If there are murders, what sort of murders and which weapons are used? These are the kinds of analytical considerations that lead to an understanding of the real meaning of violent episodes in the cinema of a particular nation in a specific era.

In popular French films of the 1920s the source of danger is always precisely defined. There is no question as to who is the culprit and little development of suspense. The most popular French films of the decade included no detective movies, no whodunits. Often the villain in French popular films is portrayed as an outright brute, whether it be Ragu in *Travail* (1919), Rollin in *La Mendiante de Saint-Sulpice* (1924), Lau in *Le Miracle des loups* (1924), Mlle. Benazer in *Les deux gamines* (1920), or Alerof in *Paris* (also 1924). The same is true of the long-lost wretched father of Berlingot in *Enfant des Halles*, the mean Russian major in *Joueur d'échecs*, the abusive chief prosecutor in *La Passion et la mort de Jeanne d'Arc*, and the nameless archetypal brute in *Coeur fidèle*. The brute is big and aggressive; his choice victims are innocents, defenseless children, women, and, of course, orphans. In other French films of the decade in which the villain is not cut to the mold of the brute, it is nonetheless always a single character who is up to no good. Evil in these French films is never nameless or faceless. In *Violettes impériales* the evildoer is Violetta's own brother gone bad, the wild-eyed anarchist. The prime mover in all things evil in *Les trois mousquetaires* (1921) is Cardinal Richelieu. In *Taô* it is the half-breed criminal of that same name.[37] In *L'Atlantide* (1921) it is the seductive temptress from whose name the film title comes. In *Napoléon* it is the rabble-rouser and English agent Paoli.

The portrayal of the single villain takes its meaning from the French situation of the 1920s. For all practical purposes France had only one enemy: a clear and recognizable source of potential danger, Germany. The characterization of the brute in these films reinforces this interpretation: France as orphan, France as abandoned and up against it, hence Germany as brute.[38]

Another element typical to the handling of violence on the French screen during the 1920s is the blood the viewer sees. Its meaning is not to be disregarded. In films about World War I blood is a common and hardly unexpected visual motif: *J'Accuse, Chignole, La grande épreuve*. The same is true of those other films that portray either wars or scenes from wars: *La Mendiante de Saint-Sulpice, La merveilleuse Vie de Jeanne d'Arc, Napoléon*, and *La Bataille*.

More precise and illuminating visual references to blood can be drawn from other films. In *Rose France* the young American Marshall Dudley Gold goes to a fortuneteller to find out if the patriotic French girl Franciane really loves him. Not insignificantly, the soothsayer draws a sample of Marshall's blood and reads from it of Franciane's passionate love for poor suffering France. When Joan of Arc, in the Theodore Dreyer film about her trial and persecution, is finally forced into a confession by her interrogators, she must submit to a bleeding. In *Le Miracle des loups* the villain Lau tricks Robert Cottereau into firing on his own true love Jeanne; in the last scenes of the film, however, Robert and a blood-covered Jeanne are reunited in a loving embrace. At the end of *Les deux gamines* the long-lost father of Ginette and Gaby is reunited with them. He had led a wretched criminal life. In the last reel he reforms. He offers blood to a dying hospital patient. It is a noble sacrifice, and as the doctors finish bleeding him, a title tells the viewer that Manin has been morally regenerated. He dies peacefully, a hero born of this sacrifice. In *L'Homme du large*, when the young man who has gone bad robs the meager savings of his poor family, his sister attempts to stop him. In so doing, she is cut on the arm and bleeds copiously. A sequence of close-up and medium shots emphasizes her bleeding as she raises her hand to cross herself, symbolizing her decision to enter a nunnery to atone for the sins of her brother. In *Coeur fidèle*, when the crippled girl shoots the villain, he falls dead beside a baby's crib. A medium shot captures the joyous face of the baby and the blood-covered face of the slain brute in the same frame. In *Les Exploits de Mandrin* the evil Bournet d'Erpigny, who has nefariously seen to it that Mandrin is hanged in spite of the King's reprieve, is found stabbed to death, his shirt soaked in blood. In *Violettes impériales*, little Violetta emerges blood splattered from the Empress's carriage after her own anarchist brother has bombed it. Blood flows, too, in *Jocelyn, Geneviève, Joueur d'échecs, Taô, Travail*, and *Le Secret du "Lone Star."*

Violence can be dramatized in the cinema without a trace of blood being actually seen. This is emphatically the case in the films of other countries during the 1920s in which blood is rarely, if ever, shown on the screen.[39] That blood is repeatedly seen in French popular films is a minor detail; a minor detail, however, only on the surface level. On the unconscious level the blood seen represents the French blood lost between 1914 and 1918. Proportionately, France had suffered the greatest human losses of the war. She had been bled, and she knew it. And during the 1920s the collective national psyche was obsessed with the memory of that bleeding. Commenting on the possibilities of Franco-German rapprochement toward the end of the decade, Georges Clemenceau wrote:

And when Mr. Stresemann [the German Foreign Minister] declares seriously that the "path is now open for cooperation between Germany and her neighbors," he is acting as the spokesman for the most criminal people of all history who, *having been unable to take our very last drop of blood*, now ironically offer us the privilege of reconstituting their strength at our costs.[40]

The blood that is seen in the popular French movies of the twenties relates to the theme of sacrifice in that same set of films. This theme reasserts itself repeatedly. In films such as *Geneviève*, *Jocelyn*, *Violettes impériales*, *Joueur d'échecs*, and *Les Mystères de Paris* the message of sacrifice is as strong as the orphan theme. In *L'Enfant des Halles* and *Les Misérables*, the sacrifice made by the hero is undertoned, but its presence is still significant. The notion of sacrifice is blended into the hero stories in both Joan of Arc films, in *Napoléon*, and in *Chignole*. Ellen Frendy in *Le Secret du "Lone Star"* is willing to sacrifice her own good name and even her love for her fiancé in order to save the reputation of her deceased father. Lia in *La Terre promise* is ready to sacrifice and marry a man she does not love for the good of her people, as, indeed, is Prince Sasha in *L'Education de prince* (1927). In *Taô*, Soun leaps to shield Chauvy from Taô's bullets, which strike her instead. In *La Bataille*, *Koenigsmark* (1923), and *L'Homme du large* the sacrifice occurs at the end of the film when in each case the heroine decides to forsake her own happiness for a loved one. In *J'Accuse* and *La grande épreuve*, both heroes, Jean Diaz and the soldier Paul, respectively, rise to the occasion and sacrifice themselves against great odds. In *Les deux gamines* Manin makes the supreme sacrifice of his own life to help another man and in so doing earns his own redemption as a human being.

In the films cited, the sacrifice is always worth it—always, in some way, rewarded. What is repeatedly portrayed in all these instances of sacrifice is epitomized in the scenes of the "raising of the dead" in Abel Gance's *J'Accuse*.[41] French soldiers lying dead on the battlefield are resurrected. They march forward and confront their relatives and friends. Then they return to those various positions of death on the battlefield from which they miraculously rose. Each one of those soldiers now knows that his death "has served a grand sacrifice." The recurrence of the theme of

sacrifice in various popular French films of the 1920s reflects the ongoing group obsession with the notion that
France had made a noble sacrifice as a nation in World War
I, and that the sacrifice had been worthwhile. Here the
wish fulfillment in the set of celluloid dreams comes closest
to merging with the mythological. France's role in World
War I was in no way "sacrificial." That it was, however, is
precisely what the French group mind wanted to believe.
France had entered the war in 1914 hoping for a swift victory and sweet rewards. Instead, the fighting bogged down
within her own frontiers, and the war of attrition that followed cost her dearly. After 1918 in many quarters in
France the view was held that France had won the war but
not the victory, that Germany had come out better than she
should have and France worse off.[42] Things turned sour.
The promised German reparations went mostly unpaid.
The alliances that were to assure France's future security
disintegrated. The unconscious wish of the French group
mind as revealed through analysis of the country's most
popular native-produced films was that she, the abandoned orphan, the old true lover, the good heroine, should
be recognized for what she was, whence would follow the
happiness and sense of security that she deserved. The
claim on that recognition was based in the myth of France's
sacrifice in the war. The group mind wanted to believe in
"France, yesterday the soldier of God, today the soldier of
humanity, always the soldier of the ideal."[43] Thus, in her
native-produced film dreams France unconsciously per-
petuated the myth that her role in World War I had been
one of sacrifice rather than merely one of suffering. This
was a mode for working off the collective national trauma
born of France's immediate postwar disappointments.

Only five French-produced films set in World War I attained broad popularity with the national audience during
the 1920s. These movies were *Chignole*, *La grande épreuve*,
J'Accuse, *Rose France*, and *Verdun*, *visions d'histoire*.

Another half-dozen films handle dramatic material dealing with some other war: *La Bataille, Joueur d'échecs, La Mendiante de Saint-Sulpice, La merveilleuse Vie de Jeanne d'Arc, Le Miracle des loups,* and *Napoléon.* Three other films contain direct references to the First World War: *La Nouvelle aurore, Les deux gamines,* and *Koenigsmark.* In all these cases references to World War I or to some other war are overt and undisguised. More revealing are the disguised references to France's wartime experience of 1914–18. Shortly after the premiere of Theodore Dreyer's *La Passion et la mort de Jeanne d'Arc* in 1927, an English reviewer commented:

> To any who have an historical, political, sociological, or even a logical flair, Joan [the Dreyer film] will be a failure. We are tired of seeing the war anyhow, but how insufferable it would be if we saw it tricked out in a romanticism that made it just a sensation to wring our hearts. So with Joan.[44]

Intriguing it would have been had the author of those lines elaborated on that odd half sentence: "We are tired of seeing the war anyhow . . ." Elaborate he did not, but the meaning of those words can only be that the Dreyer film, featuring hobgoblinish prosecutors who abuse and persecute the innocent, childlike, abandoned heroine Joan, is a parable of World War I. The association between the Joan of Arc story and the First World War is drawn directly in Marco de Gastyn's *La merveilleuse Vie de Jeanne d'Arc.* Joan's childhood friend, Rémy Loiseau, who had carried her standard, falls in battle. Later, Joan goes to his grave to pray. As she kneels, the tombstone inscription changes visually before the movie viewers eyes:

Rémy Loiseau, Royale Lorraine, Rocroy, 1643
Rémy Loiseau, Garde française, Fontenoy, 1745
Rémy Loiseau, 3ème demi-brigade, Valmy, 1792
Rémy Loiseau, 1ère Voltigeurs, Montmirail, 1814
Rémy Loiseau, 156ème d'infanterie, Verdun, 1916

The reference here to an actual recent event in national history is blunt, primitive, and rare. It is not the manner in which references to the shared, collective national experience normally occur in cinematographic dreams.

The manner in which national events and their consequences are reflected in the popular cinema is oblique, disguised, and unconscious. The attempt here has been to unravel and decipher the meaning of some repetitive themes and motifs in French popular films of the 1920s. Historical and psychological categories of analysis have been interwoven to get at the mass, public meaning of some of the symbols and images of French films that most appealed to the mass audience. This process discloses both overt and disguised references to the shared national trauma of World War I and its immediate postwar consequences for France as a whole.[45]

NOTES

1. See the discussion of films and their plots in Bela Balazs, *Der sichtbare Mensch, eine Film-Dramaturgie* (Halle: no date), 2. Aufl., pp. 35–57; Robert Gessner, *The Moving Image* (New York: 1968); Roy Huss and Norman Silverstein, *The Film Experience* (New York, Evanston, and London: 1968), pp. 127 ff.; Ernest Lindgren, *The Art of the Film* (London: 1948), pp. 35–47; Rod Whitaker, *The Language of Film* (Englewood Cliffs: 1970), pp. 139 ff.
2. Ricardo Canudo, *L'Usine aux Images* (Geneva: 1927), p. 87.
3. Other national cinemas have, of course, produced orphan films. The American cinema of the 1920s was, in fact, fond of the genre. But those American orphan films differed in detail and impact from the French counterparts and were also not so exceptionally popular in the total context of American production.
4. By comparison, the German cinema hardly ever portrayed children. Of 63 films for the years 1919–29 that could be documented as exceptionally popular with German audiences, only three have any child actors, and in these children are depicted as being threatened.
5. Carl Vincent, *Histoire de l'art cinématographique* (Brussels: no date), p. 21. Cited also in René Jeanne and Charles Ford, *Histoire en-*

cyclopédique du cinema (Paris: 1947), pp. 338, 339, and in Georges Sadoul, Histoire du cinéma français (Paris: 1962), p. 32.

6. Otto Rank, The Myth of the Birth of the Hero (New York: 1964), pp. 65, 66.

7. Ibid., p. 72.

8. Sigmund Freud, The Interpretation of Dreams, trans. and ed. by James Strachey (New York: 1965), pp. 435 ff.; also, Rank, op cit., p. 73.

9. Henri Agel, Miroir de l'insolite dans le cinéma français (Paris: 1958), p. 99.

10. Sadoul, op. cit., pp. 24, 25.

11. The Germans, for example, produced very few films incorporating landscape passages. See Ludwig Kapeller, "Die deutsche Landschaft als Filmbühne," Die Lichtbildbühne, no. 13, 29 March 1919, pp. 30–32; Robert Spa, "Dans les studios de Berlin," Ciné-Miroir, 7ème année, no. 147, 27 January 1928, no page number; Siegfried Kracauer, From Caligari to Hitler (Princeton: 1947), p. 75.

12. Emile Roux-Parassac, "Le Studio France," Ciné-Miroir, 7ème année, no. 176, 17 August 1928, pp. 535 ff.; "Les Films tournés au Maroc," Ciné-Miroir, 4ème année, no. 82, 1 September 1925, pp. 275, 276.

13. Kenneth MacPherson, "As Is," Close-Up, vol. I, no. 1, July 1927, p. 8.

14. Henri Fescourt et al., Le Cinéma: des origines à nos jours (Paris: 1932), pp. 154, 155.

15. La Petite Illustration, no. 408, supplément cinématographique, no. 14, 24 November 1928, p. 10.

16. H. A. Potamkin, "Le Cinéma américain et l'opinion française." La Revue du cinéma, 1ère série, no. 4, 15 October 1929, p. 56.

17. One of the few exceptions to this rule among France's most popular films was Un Chapeau de paille d'Italie, directed by René Clair.

18. Elie Fauré, Fonction du cinéma (Geneva: 1964), p. 29. The same notion is expressed in different form in Canudo, op. cit., p. 37.

19. Le Courrier cinématographique, 19ème année, no. 4, 29 January 1928, p. 9. That other foreign audiences reacted in much the same way as the Norwegians is confirmed in O. B., "Vision d'histoire," Close-Up, vol. II, no. 2, Feburary 1928, p. 20.

20. Agel, op. cit., p. 99.

21. Freud, op. cit., p. 435.

22. Ludovic Nadeau, La France se regarde: le problème de la natalité (Paris: 1931), p. 443.

23. Michel Huber, Henri Bunlé, and Ferdnand Boverat, La Population de la France: son évolution et ses perspectives (Paris: 1950), p. x.

24. Nadeau, op. cit., p. 10; Huber, Bunlé, and Boverat, op. cit., pp. 10, 11; Armand Armengaud, La Population française au XXème siècle (Paris: 1965), p. 8.

25. Jacques Chastenet, Les Années d'illusions, 1918–1931 (Paris: 1960), pp. 15, 16.

26. Ibid., pp. 14–16.

27. Armengaud, op. cit., pp. 16, 17.

28. *Ibid.*, pp. 18, 19. A detailed description of the evolution of the birth rate is found in Philippe Ariés, *Histoire des populations françaises et leur attitudes devant la vie depuis le 18ème siècle* (Paris: 1948), pp. 386–427, 461–70.

29. Jacqueline Beaujeu-Garnier, *La Population française* (Paris: 1969), p. 9.

30. Nadeau, *op. cit.*, p. 5.

31. *Bonsoir* (Paris), 9 August 1923, p. 4.

32. Fernand L'Hullier, *De la Sainte-Alliance au pacte atlantique* (Neuchatel: 1955), II, pp. 139, 160 ff. See also Chastenet, *op. cit.*, pp. 79 ff. For an interesting discussion of England's attitude toward German reparations payments, see Carl Bergmann, *The History of Reparations* (Boston and New York: 1927).

33. Pierre Renouvin, *Histoire des relations internationales: "les crises du XXème siècle"* (Paris: 1957), I, pp. 191 ff.; Frederick L. Schuman, *War and Diplomacy in the French Republic* (New York and London: 1931), pp. 253 ff.; Charles Petrie, *Diplomatic History* (London: 1948), pp. 33, 332. Also, Arno J. Mayer, *Politics and Diplomacy of Peacemaking: Containment and Counterrevolution at Versailles 1918/1919* (New York: 1967); Ivo J. Lederer, *The Versailles Settlement* (Boston: 1967). An interesting Marxist interpretation of the French falling out with England is found in W. J. Potjomkin, *Geschichte der Diplomatie* (Berlin: 1948), I, pp. 114 ff.

34. Of particular interest are several French monographs written during the 1920s on this subject: Charles Gautier, *L'Angleterre et nous* (Paris: 1922); Alcide Ebray, *A Frenchman Looks at the Peace*, trans. by E. W. Dickes; Henri Brenier, *French Points of View*, trans. by the author. (Marseilles: 1921). See also *Les Délibérations du Conseil de Quatre* (24 Mars–28 Juin, 1919), notes de l'Officier Interprète Paul Mantoux (Paris: 1955), II.

35. In a handful of French popular films the dream-wish is distorted with regard to the actual reuniting of the lovers. Instead, there is an emotional or psychological reuniting that reinforces the wish fulfillment in the more typical movies. These films are: *La Bataille, Koenigsmark, La Légende de soeur Beatrix, Maldone, Les Trois mousquetaires, and La Valse de l'adieu.*

36. L'Hullier, *op. cit.*, p. 139.

37. The only exception might be found in the film *Taô*; but the "evil spirit" is quickly revealed to be a man named Taô. The story of *Atlantide* is curious and develops some suspense, but the source of danger is, nonetheless, clear.

38. During the war itself Allied propaganda persistently portrayed the Germans as brutish—Huns who raped women and butchered babies. That the image of the "Boche" as brute carried over into French popular films in the 1920s in disguise is not surprising.

39. German popular films of the same decade, for example, scrupulously avoided the showing of blood. See Chapter Five, pp. 130–133.

40. Georges Clemenceau, *Grandeurs et misères d'une victoire* (Paris: 1930), pp. 329, 330. The author's italics.

41. *J'Accuse* is often considered to be a pacifist film. See René Jeanne, "Les Metteurs en scene français: Abel Gance," *Ciné-Miroir*, 2ème année, no. 22, 15 March 1923, p. 86; Kevin Brownlow, *The Parade's Gone By* (London: 1969), pp. 533 ff., as well as other sources. In fact, the film glorifies the idea of the value of sacrifice in war. For a discussion of how rarely pacifism is really represented in feature films, see Michael Radtke, "Irrwitzige Schlachten: Ein Film Anti-Krieg ist kein Film Anti-Krieg," *Film und Fernsehen*, 9. Jahrg., no. 5, May 1917, pp. 15–19.

42. Louis Forest, "Pourqoui les Allemands ne se semblent pas vaincus," *Le Matin* (Paris), 2 January 1919, p. 2. Articles in this vein were so common in French newspapers in the years immediately following World War I that a survey of any one for a given period will yield examples. Magazines published numerous articles along the same lines, including the film-industry trade journals. In this last category, see, for example, P. Simonot, "Achevons la victoire," *La Cinématographie française*, 2ème année, no. 13, 1 February 1919, pp. 3, 4 or *Le Courrier cinématographique*, 10ème année, no. 39, 25 September 1920, which editorialized: "Don't do a thing my friends, just go on living. Germany will pay. You are the victors—dance! And you danced, and you're still dancing. But it's not Germany that is paying, it's us."

43. Chastenet, *op. cit.*, pp. 13, 14.

44. Kenneth Macpherson, "As Is," *Close-Up*, vol. III, no. 1, July 1928, p. 9.

45. Two French film historians have written that at the end of World War I "France continued to exploit, though perhaps less forcefully, the themes that were popular before the war," Maurice Bardech and Robert Brasillach, *Histoire du cinéma* (Paris: 1966), p. 201. The statement is misleading. On the latent level the discoveries of this research indicate that much of the disguised material in French popular films of the 1920s refer to the aftermath of the war itself. And even on the overt, manifest level French films of the 1920s differed from the primitive science-fiction fantasies of George Méliès, the comedies of Max Linder and Prince Rigadin, or the adventure mysteries of Louis Feuillade. On the other hand, the persistence of the theme of isolation and abandonment evidently persisted in French films right up to the eve of World War II. This is suggested in Raymond W. Whitaker, *The Content Analysis of Film: A Survey of the Field, An Exhaustive Study of "Quai des Brumes," and a Functional Description of the Film Language*, unpublished dissertation, Northwestern University, Evanston, 1966, pp. 254 ff.

5

German Movies and the Obsessions of a Nation

Elements and techniques of cinematographic impressionism were frequently integrated into the popular, commercial films of France during the 1920s. In Germany during the same decade, although only a few of the true expressionist films achieved broad popularity,[1] the influence of expressionistic devices in numerous films is noticeable. For example, light and shadow play an inordinately important visual role in these German films. Even among contemporaries, the German cinema was known for its morbidity[2] and was cited for its capacity to psychologically "uproot" the viewer.[3] Expressionist elements lent themselves to a cinema that seemed bent on distortion, pathology, and alienation. Rather than recreating reality, German directors often seemed to be striving for a kind of "hyper-reality,"[4] and common to the Weimar screen was a sense of introspection and subjectivity that is not found in the silent movies of other countries.[5]

[115]

One contemporary foreign critic characterized the cinema of Weimar Germany as emphasizing a "watchfulness" that harked upon "claustrophobia."[6] That claustrophobia found its corollary in the fact that during the 1920s German film-makers remained steadfastly bound to studio production.[7] The French cinema of the decade was narrative, descriptive, and objective. The German directors, by contrast, were the first in the history of the motion picture to integrate settings with the thematic content of a film.[8] It was in Germany, also, that the use of a "moving" camera to portray a filmed sequence subjectively was perfected.[9] In 1924 the cameraman for *Der letzte Mann*, Karl Freund, created a scene depicting drunkenness by strapping a camera to his chest and staggering about the set.[10] The German film-makers of the 1920s were the masters of the techniques by which objects and events were shown on the screen as if seen through the eyes of a character in the film rather than being observed "objectively" from the camera's neutral vantage point. The creation of a subjective mood and the resulting immersion of the viewer into a film's psychodramatic contents were reinforced by the tendency of German film-makers to use descriptive titles sparingly or to omit them altogether.[11] The composition of German films was fast paced and sometimes emphasized "parts of the body or objects captured from different angles."[12] The final effect on the viewer was a kind of haunting disorientation created by the visual obsession with "curious details."[13]

Of the over 60 German films that can be documented as having enjoyed widespread, nationwide popularity between 1919 and 1929, some 40 of them deal with a story of "betrayal." An outright betrayal or an abuse of confidence, moreover, typically leads to a tragedy or a disaster in these movies. Several of the most powerful treatments of this theme are found in films that deal with the Napoleonic invasion of German territories. To begin at the end of the decade, in *Andreas Hofer* (1929), the young Tirolean bride Moidl, sensing that her new husband is going to warn the French invaders that the Tiroleans plan an uprising, confronts him and pleads: "Don't betray us!" He intends to do so in spite of her plea but never gets a chance. Moidl shoots him dead on the spot, and that shot sparks the Tirolean uprising. The rebels, led by Andreas Hofer, are singularly successful until they are "betrayed" by the Austrian government, which had promised them aid. And this betrayal, at the governmental level is, in turn, compounded by the treachery of a local farmer who, for a reward, reveals the hiding place of Andreas Hofer. Hofer is captured and executed by the French. *Die elf Schillschen Offiziere* (1926) portrays a similar story, centering around a group of "free booters" led by Ferdinand von Schill. Schill was the leader of a band of renegades who resisted the Napoleonic invasion after the Prussian monarch had signed the humiliating Peace of Tilsit.[14] In the film the lot of them are betrayed by a wealthy landowner named Mallwitz who reports their hiding place to the French. Napoleon orders the rebels shot. In *Der Katzensteg* (1927) the "Master of Schanden"[15] sends his daughter to do the dirty work of leading French invaders through a hidden pass in the mountain called the "Katzensteg." The result is defeat for the Prussians and a curse that falls upon the heads of the children of the Master of Schanden who suffer greatly. In *Waterloo* (1929) the drama concerns the intrigues of Napoleon's wily agent the Countess Tarnowska, who betrays the friendship of a Prussian lieutenant to steal the military plans for an attack against the French. She gets these plans to Napoleon through the instrumentality of a Prussian turncoat who delivers them. A more oblique and displaced reference to the betrayal theme as associated with the Napoleonic wars is found in *Der alte Fritz* (1927). Much of the film's plot revolves around Frederick the Great's concerns about the weaknesses of his designated successor. In the final scenes of the movie, in what might be considered gratuitous passages "tacked on" to the story of Frederick the Great, Napoleon is shown standing in the year 1806 at Frederick's grave. He explains that he would not be there were Frederick still alive. The implication is clear. Frederick's successor has indeed betrayed the legacy of the dynasty by failing to live up to the confidence placed in him to preserve the Prussian greatness that Frederick had established.

Interestingly, all these films dealing with the era of the Napoleonic wars were most popular in the last few years of the 1920s. Apparently, in what was agreed to be a more stable period for Germany than the earlier years of the decade, a certain resentment against the French persisted. But overt resentment against the French was not the main point of these films. Their message is the more subtle one involving the notion of betrayal. This message, indeed, is found in many of the German films of the 1920s that have since been cited elsewhere repeatedly as having contributed to the development of the film as art. In *Faust* (directed by F. W. Murnau, 1926) the theme of the abuse of confidence is clear. Faustus screams at Mephisto toward the end of the film, "You have betrayed me, for she suffers," referring to Gretchen who is being unjustly burned at the stake. In Paul Wegener's *Der Golem, wie er in die Welt kam* (1920) it is the rabbi's daughter sleeping with the Christian Florian that represents a betrayal of her boy friend and of the whole Jewish community. So enraged is the boy friend, the rabbi's assistant, at this, that in his anger he sets the great robot "The Golem" into action; it runs amuck, nearly destroying the city. In Fritz Lang's *Metropolis* (1927) a complicated form of betrayal likewise leads to the near destruction of an entire city. The wily inventor Rotwang makes a robot in the image of the working-class girl Maria, who has preached peaceful resistance to the downtrodden worker-slaves of the futuristic city. Her robot image betrays these teachings and leads the workers into a wild riot that almost results in the obliteration of the workers' city itself.[16] The film version of *Der Student von Prag* (1926), directed by Henrik Galeen, concerns the student Balduin, who sells his soul to the devil. To be precise, he trades his mirror image for wealth. In the course of the film Balduin, the best fencer in Prague, promises to spare an opponent. Balduin, intending to keep the promise, arrives late at the duel site, finds his opponent dead, and sees his own image—sword in hand—fleeing the scene. The betrayal here is unique: Balduin has been double-crossed by his own image, his alter ego. Calamity and catastrophe follow, and Balduin's life becomes a shambles. E. A. Dupont's *Variété* (1925) likewise deals with personal disloyalty—indeed, twice over. The carnival trapeze artist "Boss" leaves his simple, modest wife to run off with the adventuresome Berthe-Marie. And, in turn, Berthe-Marie takes up with the internationally known Artinelli. This affair ends with the "Boss" killing his rival.

The triangle story in the German cinema is fraught with a sense of disloyalty and treachery, which, as the reader knows by now, was not the case in French films during the same period. The German films repeatedly rework the theme of betrayal and an abuse of confidence leading to tragedy. This is as true in *Alkohol* (1919) as it is in *Asphalt*, which premiered a full decade later. In *Geschlecht in Fesseln* (1928) and in *Graf Cohn* (1923) the revelation of unfaithfulness leads to the suicide of the protagonist in both films. In *Ich hab' mein Herz in Heidelberg verloren* (1926) it results in a tragic duel in which a young student is fatally wounded. And the Prince of Eschnapur takes such revenge on his wife's lover in *Das indische Grabmal* (1921) that the poor woman is driven to kill herself.[17]

Lady Hamilton (1921) portrays the social rise of Emma Lyon, who marries Lord Hamilton, with a double reference to betrayal. In one segment of the film the treacherous Neapolitan named Cariciollo betrays his king and leads a rebellion. Lord Admiral Nelson knows how to deal with traitors and has Cariciollo first hanged and "then thrown to the fishes." The second disloyalty is on the personal level. Lady Hamilton becomes pregnant, and her husband calculates correctly that the child cannot be his. He expels her from his house and disowns her from his will. In the final scenes of the film she walks through the streets of London—baby in her arms—impoverished, heartbroken, and humiliated. There is a comparable combination of the themes of public and personal betrayal in *Madame Du Barry* (1919). The story of Madame Du Barry, her lover Armand de Foix, and her affair with King Louis XV intertwines both personal and political treachery, deceit, and abuse of confidence in a complex plot.

In Part II of *Die Nibelungen* (1924) called "Krimhilde's Revenge," Etzel has the great hall set afire once his guests the Burgundians are inside it. Thus is Krimhilde's revenge against Hagen and the other Burgundians for the murder of Siegfried carried out on the basis of a betrayal of their trust. In a film that develops at an entirely different dramatic level, *Prinz Kuckkuck* (1919), a young man inherits millions. His own cousin spirits him off on a grand tour of Europe. They arrive in Sicily where a thug is hired to kill the young heir so that the cousin and other relatives can inherit the money. Prinz Kuckkuck, however, defends himself neatly from the assailant's attempted stab in the back and in a rage hurls his treacherous cousin off a cliff.

Material related to the betrayal theme is so persistent in German popular films of the 1920s that it often assumes oblique, displaced forms. In *Anna Boleyn* (1920) the betrayer is betrayed. Anna leaves her lover to take up with King Henry VIII. From having given birth to Henry's child, she awakens to find him kissing another woman. The King then compounds Anna's misery by forcing a young man to confess to having had sexual relations with her. On the basis of this trumped-up betrayal she is beheaded. In *Der Mann ohne Namen* (1921) Pol kills his boss Palma and escapes with embezzled money. This double-cross between thieves occurs against the background of a workers' revolt against Palma, whose firm has been discovered to be a swindle based on a clever abuse of confidence. In *Dr. Mabuse, der Spieler* (1922) the betrayal element enters the complicated plot when the gambler Mabuse has a riot staged so that one of his own henchmen who has been arrested can be gunned down. Mabuse fears that the man will betray his identity to the police, and so he has him eliminated. The weasel of an impresario in *Mädchenhandel* (1926) betrays the trust of a young girl in his employ and hustles her off to a mob of white slavers, and the chief criminal in *Spione* (1928), a man named Haghi, orders a bank building gassed so that he can escape the police as his cronies and henchmen are being asphyxiated.

In five of the most popular films of the decade the notion of betrayal is only illusory or imagined. In *Die Buddenbrooks* (1923), as the family business and the world that is built upon it begin to crumble, the oldest and most responsible of the family's scions becomes obsessed with the vision of his wife having an affair with her music teacher. Only after much agonizing over the matter is Thomas convinced by the music teacher that his imagination is playing dirty tricks on him.[18] In *Danton* (1922) the hero is finally trapped by Robespierre's followers on the pretense that he is betraying the revolution. In *Die Frau im Mond* (1929) matchsticks are drawn to decide which one of the excursion party must stay behind on the moon because the spaceship's fuel reserves are nearly exhausted. Windigger draws the shortest matchstick and promptly feels himself betrayed by the others because he was opposed to the trip from the very beginning. In the final scenes, however, his fiancée Frieda steals away from the spaceship to remain with him on the moon. When a British climbing team conquers a mountain in *Der Kampf ums Matterhorn* (1928), all fall to their deaths except the leader Whymplier. When he returns safely to the village at the foot of the Matterhorn, the townspeople accuse him of having betrayed his fellow climbers to save himself. A native of the town named Anton—though he thinks of himself as Whymplier's competitor—does not believe the accusations. Anton climbs the mountain and brings back a torn rope as proof positive that Whymplier did not cut the rope to survive.[19] In *Kreuzzug des Weibes* (1926) a state's attorney suspects that his fiancée has been unfaithful to him when she becomes pregnant. In anger and bitterness he leaves her, only to discover shortly thereafter that she had actually been raped by a mentally disturbed young man. Yet another elaboration on the betrayal motif occurs in *Frühlings Erwachen* (1929). Moritz Siefel is expelled from school for possessing a diary that details experiences the school officials consider improper for adolescents. The notebook actually belongs to Moritz's classmate Melchior. But Moritz chooses not to betray his friend by revealing the identity of the real author of the diary. After his expulsion from the school, Moritz commits suicide.

Represented in various forms, the betrayal theme is the most important single characteristic of German popular films in the 1920s. The association of betrayal to disaster is significant in these movies, and the instances in which a foreigner appears as a harbinger of catastrophe in them are likewise striking. *Der alte Fritz* ends on a grim note, with the invader Napoleon standing at Frederick the Great's grave. In *Andreas Hofer* the French bring disaster with them, as they do in *Die elf Schillschen Offiziere* and *Der Katzensteg* as well. More subtle is the fact that in *Asphalt* the tragedy of the drama is betokened by the arrival of the "Consul," a foreigner, back in Berlin. And more subtle yet is the illusory betrayal in *Die Buddenbrooks*, which centers around Thomas's fears that his wife is cheating on him with her music teacher, a foreigner named Throata.

In *Das indische Grabmal* the love affair of his wife and

the foreign officer Mac Allen provokes the Prince of Eschnapur to revenge, which ends tragically. In *Mädchenhandel*, which is subtitled "An International Danger," the
white slavers are all swarthy-looking foreigners. The film
concludes with a "factual" warning to German girls against
accepting jobs in foreign countries. It is the nefarious deal-
ings of the foreign thugs, first Palmas and then the vil-
lainous Pol, that furnish the plot for *Der Mann ohne Namen*.
In *Prinz Kuckkuck* a Sicilian is hired to murder the lovable
Teutonic hero. In the Harry Piel adventure film *Rivalen*
(1923) the evildoer is a foreigner named Ravallo. In *Variété*
it is the disruptive intrusion of the foreigner Artinelli into
the lives of "Boss" and Berthe-Marie that spells tragedy. The
prime villain in *Waterloo* is Napoleon's agent, the foreign
Countess Tarnowska.[20]

In *Wolga-Wolga* (1928) the Persian Princess Zanielle's
coming on board the rebel ship of Stenka Rasin harkens
the beginning of a tragic ending. Zanielle is not only a
foreigner ("Ausländerin") but also a foreign element
("Fremde"). Rasin himself had established a rule that no
women would be allowed on board the ship; he breaks that
very rule out of his love for Zanielle. A parallel associative
transition from foreigner to foreign element (i.e., outsider)
exists in other films as well. In the German popular cinema
of the 1920s foreigners and persons who are outsiders share
a common dramatic function—their arrival on the scene
betokens impending danger and disaster. The sudden, mys-
terious appearance of Scapinelli in *Der Student von Prag*,
like the similar emergence of Mephisto in *Faust*, signals
imminent tragedy. Both are foreign elements in the world
into which they have come, as is the character who represents death in *Der müde Tod* (1920), who, indeed, is known
in the film only as "Der Fremde." In *Nosferatu* (1921) the
foreigner who is also a foreign element is a carrier of death.
The vampire Count Nosferatu comes out of the East, spreading plague in his wake as he travels to the German city of

Bremen. The blame for all evil in *Metropolis* falls in the end on the strange magician Rotwang, although the logic of the film would indicate that the ruler of the city, Fredersen, is equally guilty. Rotwang lives in an old house, with thatched roof and a star decorating the door, in the midst of an ultramodern city of rulers and worker-slaves. Rotwang fits into neither category; he is the single "outsider" in the futuristic city. In another film by the same director, Fritz Lang, the lurking danger of the foreign element is pinpointed by one of the characters. Countess von Toll in *Dr. Mabuse, der Spieler* enters a crowded gambling casino and remarks: "There is a foreign element in our midst tonight." The foreign element is Mabuse, a wily genius of many disguises, hypnotic talents, and underworld connections. In due course, the "foreign element" strikes that very night, and a man named Hull is murdered at Mabuse's secret bidding.

The pattern is clear. In popular German films of the 1920s tragedy is repeatedly precipitated when an outsider intrudes where he or she does not belong. In both *Der Berg des Schicksals* (1924) and *Der Kampf ums Matterhorn*, danger is imminent when foreigners arrive to try to conquer great mountains, which fascinate the villagers who live at the foot of them. In *Wettlauf ums Glück* (1923) the arrival of two Europeans in a Chinese hamlet in which Pastor Helmer and his daughter have been long established harkens impending tragedy. In *Der Golem, wie er in die Welt kam* catastrophe follows the intrusion of Florian, a Christian emissary of the Emperor, into the Jewish ghetto. Here the outsider motif is being elaborated twice over, for the Jews themselves are already a "foreign element" living as a community in Christian Prague. The Jew as outsider is the very core of the film entitled *Graf Cohn*. In it, the intrusion of a Jewish merchant's son into the German aristocracy spells tragedy and costs Isidor Cohn his life. The tragedy of suicide in *Die wunderbare Lüge der Nina Petrowna* (1929)

[124]

is likewise occasioned by the intrusion of the impoverished Michael into the wealthy society in which Nina Petrowna flourishes. The films *Anna Boleyn*, *Lady Hamilton*, and *Madame Du Barry* all portray similar situations and all are set in foreign countries. In each of these movies, the heroines are social upstarts, intruders, outsiders. They have invaded levels of society to which they do not rightly belong, and this leads to catastrophe.

Beyond the characterization of the foreigner as evildoer, there is a distinct racist strain in several popular German films of the decade. This racism is particularly evident in *Die Herrin der Welt* (1919) and *Der Mann ohne Namen*. In both films Caucasian heroes do in Orientals, Arabs, and Black Africans at a frenetic pace. The demeaning of non-Europeans also enters into *Das indische Grabmal*, *Geheimnisse des Orients* (1928), and *Wettlauf ums Glück*. The Asiatic barbarism of the Huns is given undue emphasis in *Die Nibelungen*, and the Russian captors of the German soldier in *Heimkehr* are portrayed as brutish orientals. In *Spione* Asians are involved in underworld enterprises, but then so is nearly every other character in the film as well. Negroes appear frequently in the German popular films of the 1920s, usually as bowing, scraping servants or as entertainers. In an episode in *Der müde Tod* a black is a hired killer. In *Madame Du Barry* the King gives his mistress a black manservant as a wedding gift.[22]

In France, which still had extensive overseas colonial holdings in the 1920s of the sort that Germany did not have, only two of the most popular native-produced films of the decade (*L'Atlantide* and *Taô*) are set outside Europe. A racist tendency in the portrayal of non-Europeans in the French cinema for this era cannot be established. One historian of the Weimar cinema has theorized that German films of the 1920s that featured "exotic sceneries" were "space-devouring films" intended to satiate vicariously the suppressed German desire for colonial expansion.[23] Yet only four of the most popular German films of the decade following World War I—*Die Herrin der Welt, Geheimnisse des Orients, Das indische Grabmal,* and *Der Mann ohne Namen*—can be cited in support of this interpretation. There is no repetitive pattern in the German films of this era, which reflects a collective obsession with colonial expansion or the quest for "Lebensraum." The significant theme in this handful of films is not geopolitical. Rather, it is a racism that interconnects with the broader portrayal of foreigners as evildoers that is found in a fair number of German popular films of the 1920s.

The betrayal theme in the most popular films of the 1920s refers at the collective level to Germany's defeat in the war of 1914–18. The theme of the foreigner or the "foreign element" as a harbinger of catastrophe also refers to that defeat, but in a peculiar way. In spite of increasing unrest on the military front and growing hardship on the home front,[24] Germany's defeat in November 1918 came as a shock to the nation. By the end of 1917 Germany had already "half won" the war. The German victory in the East was sealed at the beginning of March 1918 with the signing of the Treaty of Brest-Litovsk.[25] That victory was extensive and unexpected. It liberated Germany from a two-front war, and the harsh terms imposed on the Soviet Russian regime meant the promise of food, fuel, raw materials in abundance, and labor for Germany. The victory marked a reversal of Russian westward expansion, which had been taking place piecemeal since the mid-eighteenth century. From the German point of view all this was no piddling matter.[26]

With half the war already won, the spring of 1918 brought Ludendorff's initially successful offensive in the West and with it hope for total victory.[27] Those hopes were dashed by late July when the offensive was halted. Yet there is no evidence that between then and the Armistice of November that the nation was prepared, either factually or psychologically, to accept the impending disaster.

Moreover, when that disaster came, there was not yet a single enemy soldier on German soil. The defeat in the West came to Germany as a shock. The force of that shock was compounded by the fact that the existence of a unified Germany had been forged through a series of Prussian military victories in the midnineteenth century. The final victory, which served to weld Germany into a nation, was in the Franco-Prussian war. The biggest winner of 1918 seemed on the surface to be France. The defeat of 1918 represented, then, the veritable reversal of the war of 1870/71 through which the German Reich had been born.

For Germany the defeat of 1918 was unanticipated and widely disbelieved. One pseudo-explanation that eventually emerged was that the nation had been "cheated" of victory. The legend of the betrayal of Germany spread quickly. In summer of 1919 Field Marshal Paul von Hindenburg appeared before a parliamentary unit set up to investigate the defeat. Hindenburg, reading a statement that had likely been prepared for him by Ludendorff, claimed the German armed forces had "been stabbed in the back."[28] Hindenburg was vague about how this had happened. He did concede that this version of the defeat had originated with an otherwise unidentified British general who had claimed that the German army had been superior to Allied forces but had been betrayed. The parliamentarians did not press Hindenburg for any further explanation.[29]

Hindenburg's testimony confirmed the betrayal legend that was already current in Germany before his appearance at the investigative hearings. That legend flourished on the basis of a double set of conditions. The psychological conditions were stipulated by the trauma of the defeat itself and the subsequent refusal to believe that it had really occurred. The factual conditions were set when an unwanted republic was called into existence in Germany on the heels of the defeat of 1918. That Weimar was a "republic without republicans" is a catch phrase that described an approximate truth. Conservatives accepted the republic only because they believed that it was the best alternative for securing an acceptable peace from the Allies.[30] Yet few Germans considered the terms of the Versailles Treaty acceptable when they were revealed. The conservatives' pragmatic compromise had backfired. At the other end of the political spectrum, the Communists did not want the republic, either—certainly not a republic grounded in the sellout of the revolution of 1918/19 by the Social Democrat "Marx-Killers."[31] And even the Social Democrats themselves, the would-be and should-be defenders of the Weimar Republic, were lukewarm in support of their own creation. Party leader Friedrich Ebert would have surely preferred a constitutional monarchy to a republic, and his feelings evidently reflected the thinking of a faction in the Social Democrat ranks.[32] What began in 1918 as a "Räte-Republik" wound up looking like a "Verräter-Republik" to almost everyone who lived under it for the next 14 years.

The recurrent theme of betrayal that has been documented from the dramatic contents of the most popular films of Weimar Germany suggests an association at the latent level to the trauma of the nation's defeat of 1918. This interpretation is reinforced by other minor themes and motifs from this same set of popular films. The first of these is the use of the clock as a leitmotif in a number of German films. In *Der alte Fritz* a giant clock looms in the background ticking away the minutes as Frederick the Great dies; the next cut is to the final scenes of the film in which Napoleon stands years later as a conqueror on German soil. In *Die Frau im Mond* the countdown before the spaceship lifts off for its doomed mission is represented by shots of a ticking clock, which is neither unusual nor conspicuous. More revealing are the repeated shots of clocks edited into the scenes of the hero first arriving in prison in *Geschlecht in Fesseln*. In *Heimkehr* at the moment Russians are about to capture a German soldier there are repeated cuts to the face of a watch. The arrival of French invaders in a German town in *Der Katzensteg* is similarly punctuated by several shots of a clock in the tower of a building on the marketplace. Films directed by Fritz Lang, which became popular with the German mass audience in the 1920's, often used the clock image. Repeated shots of a great clock mark the pandemonium of selling set off at the stock exchange in *Dr. Mabuse, der Spieler*. In *Metropolis* young Fredersen's first descent into the subterranean worker's city is visually dramatized by editing in shots of a great clock. The same motif appears in *Der müde Tod* without the use of an actual clock. When the stranger who represents death first threatens to steal a young man from his sweetheart, the stranger's shadow casts itself oddly in the form of an hourglass with the sand running out of it quickly. Toward the end of the same film, the girl's frantic attempts to save her lover from death are represented as a race against the clock—quite literally. In *Spione* the clock motif is repeated several times. The first instance is in association with the discovery that a woman had tried to murder the investigator Tremaine. A ticking clock is also shown when Tremaine propositions the wily Sonia for the first dangerous time. Later, when Sonia argues with her employer, the spy-ring leader Haghi, a strange-looking clock placed on Haghi's desk is given unusual emphasis in the scene.

In *Mutter Krausens Fahrt ins Glück* (1929), when mother Krausen turns on the gas burner to boil water for coffee, a clock pendulum is shown swinging. The clock itself then appears on the screen as mother Krausen loosens the gasline connection, thus taking her "trip into happiness" as she commits suicide. In *Nosferatu* danger is forewarned by shots of a clock, with a skeleton figure tapping away the seconds with a tiny hammer. And in *Faust* the devil persuades Faust to make a pact with him by showing an hourglass with the sands running out of it quickly. In *Variété*, when "Boss" first begins to suspect that Berthe-Marie is cheating on him with Artinelli, his torment is portrayed by his repeatedly looking at a clock. In *Die Verrufenen* (1925), as Robert Kramer tells newfound friends his tragic story of imprisonment and the hardships of life as an ex-convict, the camera cuts repeatedly to a clock on the mantle in the room.

The visual use of a clock to represent the passing of time is certainly not unique to German silent films of the 1920s. But the emphatic use of this imagery indicates its significance, and the fact that in these German films the clock usually represents impending danger or disaster rather than just the passing of time clarifies that significance. Interpretively, the clock motif refers to the lost war of 1914–18. In the single Germany cinematographic "history" of the war, a 1927 production entitled *Der Weltkrieg*, it is emphasized that the German strategy for winning a two-front war was based on the concept of "winning time" ("Zeitgewinn"). Naturally this is a simplification of a complex military plan, but it was the Germans' own simplification. Once the planned first offensive of 1914 fizzled, and the war become one of attrition, Germany was not only up against the enemy but up against the time factor.[33] Her military system was not fitted for an extended war.[34] Germany had pushed for war in 1914 because it was felt that her chances for winning an inevitable war were running down with time. According to Chancellor Bethmann Hollweg the military advised him in 1914: "Now it's still possible . . . but it won't be in two years."[35] In 1918 time ran out on Germany; she was forced to sue for peace. And though it presents a different time reference, it is possibly relevant that one of the slogans of the legend of the betrayal (or "the stab in the back") was that it took place "five minutes before the final victory."

In contrast to the blood that is seen in the popular French

films of the 1920s,[36] violence and death in German films of the same era are portrayed bloodlessly. The death of the escaped convict in *Alkohol* (1919) is bloodless; he perishes in a fire. The murder in *Geschlecht in Fesseln* is unsanguinary, as is the subsequent suicide of the unfortunate man who committed the crime. In *Anna Boleyn* the heroine is led off to be beheaded; the execution itself is not shown. The same is true of the film *Madame Du Barry*. In *Asphalt* policeman Albert Houk manages the neat trick of beating the Consul to death with the leg of a chair without any blood being seen. Dozens of non-Europeans are killed in one way or another in *Die Herrin der Welt*, but whatever the way, it is invariably bloodless.

The citing of film after film to demonstrate what was not in German movies of the 1920s tends toward ennui. Reference, however, to another handful of films will, hopefully, make clear what was involved in the bloodlessness of Weimar cinema. In *Spione* at the beginning of the movie a man is shot pointblank by one of the master spy Haghi's agents. The shooting is portrayed in a series of medium shots, but, strikingly, not a drop of blood is seen. The murder of Gretchen's brother in *Faust*, Balduin's death through the shooting of his shadow image in *Der Student von Prag*, and Frieda's killing of Turner in *Die Frau im Mond* are all likewise anemic. In *Das indische Grabmal*, Mac Allen is ripped apart by tigers, and the Princess leaps to her death from a bridge—in both cases bloodlessly. In *Der Kampf ums Matterhorn* four English climbers fall to their deaths from a mountain clean of gore. In *Die weisse Hölle von Piz Palü* another climber receives a slight gash, but Dr. Kraft freezes to death on a mountain ledge without a trace of blood. When Nine Petrowna's body is discovered after her suicide in *Die wunderbare Lüge der Nina Petrowna*, no blood is seen. In *Mutter Krausens Fahrt ins Glück* the murder of the watchman is unsanguinary, as are the deaths of mother Krausen and the little girl who is left in her care. In

Lady Hamilton the Neapolitan traitor is hanged, and the death of Lord Nelson is not shown at all, but merely reported. In *Ich hab' mein Herz in Heidelberg verloren* the death of Rudolf in a duel is reported but not seen.

Instead of blood being actually seen, there are references to blood in several popular German films of the era. In *Danton* the hero proclaims that the revolution "must drink the blood of the enemies of humanity." Ferdinand von Schill's rebel "Freikorps" members are referred to as Germany's "truebloods" in *Die elf Schillschen Offiziere*. In *Der alte Fritz* a title explains that Frederick the Great loves the Pomeranians because "they have bled for the fatherland." In the same film there is a reference to an oath "signed in blood" in which young Frederick William has made promises to his mistress Wilhelmine. Faustus, too, in film director Murnau's adaptation from Marlowe and Goethe signs an oath to Mephisto in blood. In *Dr. Mabuse, der Spieler* Countess von Toll describes the nightlife of decadent Berlin as a mad quest for stimulation "of our tired blood." In *Variété*, which is set in the same milieu as *Mabuse*, "Boss" stabs his girl friend's lover to death; no blood is seen. Then Boss returns to the room he shares with Berthe-Marie. He cleans his hands at a small sink, the viewer seeing only the water in the basin darken as Boss literally washes the blood from them. The vampire in *Nosferatu* lives off the blood of his victims, though the blood that he draws from them is itself never seen. As Nosferatu arrives in Bremen, bringing the deadily plague with him, his henchman Renfield, who has been jailed, starts receiving telepathic messages from his master and begins screaming, "Blood, blood, blood."

The blood that is unseen in German films and is nonetheless referred to represents the German blood that was drained in World War I. Germany had fought the war entirely outside her own frontiers. German soldiers fell on foreign soil and only there. The blood that was shed in the

German cause was thus "unseen" from the collective, national viewpoint. That no foreign soldier was on German soil when the war ended in November 1918 has already been cited as a factor in Germany's disbelief in the defeat. For the French the blood that had flowed between 1914 and 1918 had been worth it. For the Germans the blood that had flowed was the lost blood of an unanticipated and undigested defeat. In the 60-odd most popular German films of the 1920s there is but a single, notable exception to the bloodlessness.[37] When in Part I of *Nibelungen* Siegfried slays the dragon, a veritable river of blood flows from the beast's side. This the very exception that proves the rule. The association to the "unseen" lost blood that flowed outside Germany's own borders on the front during the war holds. For from 1914 on, and all through the war, the German front line was called the "Siegfried Line," whence "Siegfried" refers to a river of lost blood.

The betrayal theme, the clock motif, and the unseen blood of the popular German films of the 1920s all refer back to the war just past and lost.[38] The major element left hanging, then, is the characterization of the foreigner or the "foreign element" as an evil figure, a carrier of catastrophe. There would have been no reason necessarily for the collectivity to associate the evil foreigner directly with Germany's wartime enemies. In the films themselves the foreigner motif often relates structurally to the theme of betrayal. This suggests a connection, again, with the unassimilated defeat of 1918; to represent the enemy as an evildoer, however, would have been gratuitous and suggest that the loss had been assimilated, which it was not. For the theme of the foreigner as evildoer relates to the defeat, not to the conduct of the war itself.

The evil foreigner of the Weimar screen is portrayed as a character of many disguises, a trickster, a creature who is ready to strike, run, and hide. The evildoer is not always a foreigner in the strict sense of the word. Often he or she is a "foreign element," frequently an insider who is nonetheless an outsider. This formulation links up with a facet of the betrayal legend concerning Germany's defeat. The foreigner, as well as the "foreign element," of the Weimar popular cinema refers to the Jew. The characterization of the trickster, the man of many disguises, or a sneaky creature who conceals his true identity coincides with the stock anti-Semitic description of the Jew. In German films the betrayer is not quite related to the person betrayed in the manner implied: a crypto son (*Der alte Fritz*), a false cousin (*Prinz Kuckkuck*), a fiancé (*Ich hab' mein Herz in Heidelberg verloren, Kreuzzug des Weibes*, and *Die Verrufenen*), a mistress (*Variété, Die wunderbare Lüge der Nina Petrowna, Madame Du Barry*), a robot (*Metropolis*), a mirror image (*Der Student von Prag*). Often the theme of imposture enters: Mabuse (*Dr. Mabuse, der Spieler*) and Haghi (*Spione*) are both men of numerous disguises, and Faustus is transformed from an aged scholar into a young man by Mephisto's magic (*Faust*). The cover-ups are numerous, some being obvious and others quite clever: Peter Voss assumes a false identity (*Der Mann ohne Namen*), the Count who buys property in Bremen is really a vampire (*Nosferatu*), a crooked newspaper publisher hires an impostor to impersonate a world-traveling young woman (*Die Herrin der Welt*), and to save embarrassment the oil magnate Waltham passes off a girl he has met in a train to business friends as his wife (*Der blinde Passagier*, 1922). And still other cases of disguise and mistaken identity are found in *Der müde Tod* and in *Die Försterchristl* (1926). According to anti-Semitic dogma Jews were not quite what they passed themselves off to be. For example, if they were citizens of a country, they were suspected of owning other allegiances. The Jew as an outsider posing as an insider is a stock notion in the pantheon of anti-Jewish sentiments.[39]

The question is why Jews should have become the butt of so many versions of the betrayal legend. Anti-Semitism in

Germany had a long history before World War I, but then few Christian countries with a Jewish minority of any size did not have a rich anti-Semitic past. During the war itself a few members of the German military staff were known to lace their communiqués with anti-Semitic "bon mots."[40] In some quarters the Imperial government was accused of letting Germany's wartime economy fall into the hands of "an international, fatherlandless pack of traders" (which is Teutonic longhand for "Jews").[41] Before the war was over the Jewish economic advisors Ballin and Rathenau were described as having created a system for the "Jewish expropriation" of the entire German economy. After the war Otto Armin (under the pseudonym Arnold Roth) published *Die Juden in den Kriegsgesellschaften* (Munich, 1921). In it he claimed Ballin had "disloyal" relationships to persons in enemy countries during the war years and that the influential German Jew Max Warburg had collaborated with his brother Paul Warburg, who was described as being "in American state service."[42] Gustav von Schmoller, an economic advisor to Kaiser Wilhelm II, took a broader swipe at the Jewish Social Democrat Hugo Preuss, calling him "one of the leaders of the Berlin communal liberalism, which, being socially based on the might of Jewish millionaires, more or less rules the capital city."[43]

Such comments associating Jews with the betrayal of Germany and German interests are important, but their significance should not be overestimated. No purge of German Jews from positions of influence was undertaken during the war. The accusation that Jews were betrayers of Germany flourished in the Weimar years, not during the war years. The trauma of the defeat of 1918 was apparently the condition that triggered the particular character that anti-Semitism took on in Germany after 1918.

Why the Jew was associated with Germany's unassimilated defeat and hence its betrayal is a question that demands further consideration in light of other elements from the nation's most popular films. In *Asphalt,* as policeman Albert Houk escorts a young woman he has arrested for theft to her arraignment, she explains to him her motive for the crime: "If I don't pay my rent I'll be put out into the street, and I have a terrible fear of the STREET." In the title the word "STRASSE" is capitalized. The emphasis seems at first gratuitous and meaningless. It is neither. The significance, however, can be understood only in the context of a theme that persists in numerous German popular films of the era. That theme is the fear of the street. *Asphalt* is a film about the breakdown of authority. Taking its name from paving material, the film opens with the comment: "The Lord of the asphalt is the man in uniform—policeman Albert Houk." In the film *Geschlecht in Fesseln* a comparable association is made. As Franz Sommer is riding home after having been released from prison, he sees a policeman. Immediately Franz visualizes the entire episode for which he was convicted on manslaughter when a man he beat up died.

The street in German films of the 1920s is typically dark, narrow, ominous, gloomy, and a place where danger lurks.[44] Often the street is directly associated with tragedy. In *Der letzte Mann,* for example, an elderly hotel doorman is demoted to a lavatory attendant. On hearing this, he walks out onto a foggy street and imagines skyscrapers falling in upon himself. In *Nosferatu,* as the Count arrives in Bremen, he carries coffins through deserted streets to his new abode, symbolizing the plague he brings with him. In a scene that follows in the film, Nosferatu's henchman Renfield is then chased through narrow city streets by a mob of townspeople. In *Die Pest in Florenz* (1919) the final scene portrays a man playing a violin who walks through streets of the city, which are strewn with corpses. In the beginning of *Faust* there are street scenes of frightened townspeople rushing about madly in fear of the plague. At the end of the same film, Gretchen is taken through streets of jeering mobs and put to death at the stake. In *Metropolis* the streets are filled with terrified children fleeing the swelling waters after the robot Marie had induced the rioting workers to flood their own city.

In *Der Golem, wie er in die Welt kam* the great monster created by Rabbi Löw runs through city streets spreading terror and destruction. In *Der Student von Prag* the student Balduin, whose life is a shambles, rushes out into deserted streets and runs through the dark, ominous city to the cemetery where he meets his uncanny death. The scenes in *Die Verrufenen*, which most poignantly portray the misery and degradation of the unemployed ex-convict, are all street scenes. In a different manner and in a different context, the documentary film *Die Wege zur Kraft und Schönheit* (1925) portrays the street as dark and threatening, this being part of a broader portrayal of the city as dangerous and unhealthy. *Lady Hamilton* ends with the heroine walking sadly through the depressing streets of a London slum where she hears the news of her lover Nelson's death.

The viciousness of soldiers and revolutionaries who fill the streets is depicted in several German popular films of the decade: *Danton, Anna Boleyn, Madame Du Barry, Königin Luise* (1927), and *Der Katzensteg*. In *Spione* the ending comes with the scenes of police and soldiers waging street battles to drive the master spy Haghi out of his lair. These sequences are almost a cinedramatic repeat performance of the street fighting that comes at the end of *Dr. Mabuse, der Spieler* when Mabuse and his cronies attempt to fight off police and army units.

The street motif in German popular films passed through several distinct but interrelated stages of development. In general the street is portrayed as dark, gloomy, and dangerous. It is the site of crimes, where low life flourishes. More specifically, the street is the place in which order breaks down unless a figure of authority maintains it. More dramatically, the street is the place where foreign soldiers loot and pillage, and revolutionaries run riot. Finally, the street is where the forces of order hunt down criminals and their cohorts. In French films of the same decade the street is normally well lit, pleasant, and full of life.

In German movies the grim portrayal of the street and the portrayal of the city overlap. This is emphatically clear in a number of films that have already been mentioned in the discussion of the street motif: *Asphalt, Der Golem, wie er in die Welt kam, Nosferatu, Die Pest in Florenz, Lady Hamilton, Dr. Mabuse, der Spieler*, and *Die Verrufenen*. The theme asserts itself as well in *Monna Vanna* (1922). *Mutter Krausens Fahrt ins Glück* is about the poverty and degradation of life in a working-class neighborhood in Berlin. In both *Heimkehr* and *Der letzte Mann* the cityscape is played off visually with great cleverness against the tragedy of both movies. Somewhat less emphatically, the same thing occurs in *Variété*. The notion that the city corrupts surfaces in *Der alte Fritz*. And *Metropolis* is a horror show about a city of the future. *Spione* begins with this information: "Spies made the city a battlefield after the war." Finally, no characterization of the city is less appealing than that found in *Die Wege zur Kraft und Schönheit*. As a title in the film explains: "Today man is condemned to live in cities."[45]

At the group level the portrayal of the street as evil and the city as dangerous refers to the German revolution of 1918/19. The opening title from *Spione* disguises its real meaning. It was not "spies" who made the city "a battlefield after the war," but revolutionaries. Several of the films already cited deal directly with revolutions or rebellions: *Danton, Madame Du Barry, Anna Boleyn*, and *Metropolis* are among them. There is a riot against taxes in *Der alte Fritz* and a revolt by Arabs in *Die Herrin der Welt*. *Der Mann ohne Namen* and *Lady Hamilton* both feature uprisings. In *Wolga-Wolga* there is a revolution among the revolutionaries; an uprising breaks out on board the ship of the anti-Czarist rebels.

One historian of the Weimar cinema has written that *Madame Du Barry*, for example, presents "Revolutionary events as originating from psychological conflicts—the revolution is reduced to a derivative of private passions." The same writer argues that *Anna Boleyn* makes "history seem the product of a tyrant's private life" and interprets *Danton* in the same way.[46] During the 1920s, however, these same films were regarded in some countries not as portraying a certain philosophy of history but as being thinly disguised anti-French (*Danton* and *Du Barry*) and anti-English (*Anna Boleyn*) message films. On the whole, though, the latent meanings of these films are more interesting than any conscious philosophical or propagandistic aims they may reveal. An interesting piece of information supports the general interpretation of the city and street motif of these German popular films of the 1920s as associating back to the German Revolution of 1918/19. During the early 1960s, Erich Pommer, who was production chief at UFA during the 1920s, said in an interview: "*Dr. Mabuse, the Gambler* was made by Fritz Lang for me, and it made a great deal of money in Germany. *Dr. Mabuse* portrays the fight between the Sparticists and the moderates. Mabuse himself was meant to portray the Spartacists (Communists)."[47] Pommer also revealed that the uprising of the workers in *Metropolis* "was patterned after the Communist attempt to take over Bavaria."[48] Apparently, however, these references to the revolution of 1918/19 did not get through to the average German movie viewer on the conscious level. Otherwise Pommer would have had no need to explain a set of associations in these films some 40 years after they premiered and became popular in Germany.[49] If the mass audience in Germany understood the latent message of these two films, that understanding must have been at the collective, unconscious level.

The German revolution was complicated and drawn out. The initial impetus was given by mutinous soldiers and sailors,[50] and "revolutionary activity" assumed various forms during the months that followed November 1918. The revolution had two geographical focal points: Munich and Berlin. The persons and events associated with these two urban centers in 1918/19 form the core of the revolution as it was remembered into the 1920s.

On November 7, 1918 Kurt Eisner proclaimed a Bavarian Republic in Munich. Eisner was a Jew from Berlin, an adherent of a minority leftist faction of the Social Democrat party, and had been released from prison a short time before he led the Bavarian revolution. It was in Munich that the revolution first struck, and there that it went the furthest. In Munich, also, the ideological concept of a regime based on councils of workers and soldiers was taken most seriously by the revolutionary leadership. Eisner himself, however, became willing to compromise; his reward was assassination in February 1919 at the hands of a rightist student. The revolution lurched, then pushed forward again. In April 1919 Bavaria was declared a Soviet Republic. The most important leader in this new regime was another Jew, Eugen Leviné. And his favorite sidekick was Max Levien, a name that was widely assumed to be Jewish, although this was false.[51]

On November 9, 1918 the revolution had come to Berlin. The responsibilities of the government were turned over to the parliamentary leader of the Social Democrat faction, Friedrich Ebert. Almost simultaneously two Social Democrats proclaimed the republic, Philipp Scheidemann naming it "democrat parliamentary" and Karl Liebknecht announcing that the new republic was "socialist." Ebert would have likely preferred it had neither of them proclaimed anything.[52] Scheidemann's version carried historically, but not until months of trouble prevailed and the Spartacist elements gathered around Liebknecht and Rosa Luxemburg had been smashed. The Spartacist uprisings in Berlin during the week of January 5 through 12, 1919 were crushed mainly by "Freikorps" troops. Liebknecht and Luxemburg were murdered on the fifteenth, and elections for a new National Assembly took place on the nineteenth. By the first week of February the "moderates" had triumphed in the German capital.[53]

The revolutionary events were still continuing months after the Armistice of November 1918. The contents of the most popular German movies of the 1920s suggest that at the collective psychological level the defeat of 1918 and the entire range of revolutionary acts of 1918/19 were "telescoped" together in the popular imagination. As legend came to have it, the war was lost because of the revolution. The revolution betrayed the nation; it was the stab in the back that sabotaged the German army. The revolutionary tumult that followed and the "white terror" of the "Freikorps" that followed after that made the streets an ominous place of bloodshed for months. The revolution began with Eisner's proclamation of a republic. The regime that formed around him in Bavaria had a decidedly Jewish character. The impact of Eisner's Jewishness on the popular imagination should not be underestimated. The political right eventually exploited the fact, but at the end of 1918 it was centrist newspapers like the *Kölnische Volkszeitung* that wrote about "the arrogance of that vagabond invader, the racial alien Kurt Eisner."[54] The end of the protracted revolution of 1918/19 came only with the crushing of the leftists in Munich at the beginning of May 1919. The revolution, which had begun with the daring proclamation of the Jew Eisner, ended with the fall of the Soviet regime led by the Jew Leviné. In between came the dramatic high point of the revolution, the Spartacist uprising of January 1919, popularly ascribed to the Jewess Rosa Luxemburg.

During his brief tenure as leader of the Bavarian regime Kurt Eisner found time to anger the nation no end. He publicized documents from the Bavarian Foreign Ministry that he believed demonstrated Germany's guilt for having provoked the First World War.[55] The ensuing Versailles Treaty contained a clause (paragraph number 231) assigning "guilt" for the war to Germany and her partners. The guilt clause rankled the German consciousness and did so not just because paragraph 231 served as the basis of claims by the Allies for Germany to pay war reparations. Dismay and anger over the guilt clause touched almost every element of German society. And it persisted through the 1920s. When Herman Katorowicz's long and authoritative study documenting Germany's responsibility for the outbreak of the war in 1914 was ready for publication in 1927, its appearance was thwarted by the Foreign Ministry under the direction of Nobel Peace Prize winner Gustav Stresemann.[56]

At the subconscious level, the German popular films of the 1920s indicate that a strong collective obsession with the question of guilt persisted throughout the decade. *Alkohol* from the year 1919 is about an ex-convict coming clean and relating to his son's girl friend the story of how he became a murderer. In *Die Buddenbrooks* particular dramatic emphasis is placed on the final scene in which Thomas Buddenbrooks comes to his estranged wife crying: "I am guilty!" *Frühlings Erwachen*, the tragic story of Moritz Siefel's suicide after he has been expelled from school, reaches an emotional climax when at Moritz's funeral his friend Melchior screams at the school professors that they are the guilty ones. *Die Verrufenen* might well be described as a movie dealing with the difficulties of bearing guilt in a bourgeois milieu, and the same is true of *Geschlecht in Fesseln* and *Asphalt*. In *Das indische Grabmal* the Prince of Eschnapur comes to realize his guilt in having carried revenge against his wife's lover too far.

In *Variété*, which begins with scenes of "Boss" in convict garb being called to the prison warden, the substance of the film is his confession of how he came to murder the trapeze artist Artinelli. *Der Student von Prag* and *Faust* are also both centrally concerned with the issue of guilt. The same is true of *Der Kampf ums Matterhorn*, *Der Katzensteg*,

Kreuzzug des Weibes, and *Der Mann ohne Namen*. In *Metropolis* Rotwang perishes, but the wealthy ruler of the city who put him up to his dirty work is exonerated. In the final scenes of the movie all guilt on all sides is expiated as masters and workers are brought together "through love."

In *Mutter Krausens Fahrt ins Glück* the guilt of the son is borne by his mother. The final tragedy in *Wolga-Wolga* results from Stenka Rasin's culpability in breaking the law against bringing women on board the rebel ship that he himself had set down. In *Die Nibelungen* Hildebrand slays Kriemhilde because he cannot bear the thought of a woman being guilty of having brought so much havoc and tragedy into the work in her lust for avenging her husband's murder.

The concern with guilt in German films is not always direct. Sometimes it is implied in that the protagonist of the film is an outcast or criminal, a pariah of one sort or another. In the course of the eight episodes of *Die Herrin der Welt* it is revealed that the globetrotting heroine had left Europe in shame—having been involved romantically with her own father's murderer, mixed up in a financial scandal, and having had an illegitimate child who died while she was in jail. The hero of *Geschlecht in Fesseln* is an unemployed engineer who is convicted of manslaughter. The hero of *Die Verrufenen* is an ex-convict who has served time for embezzlement. The main character in *Der Bettelstudent* (1927) has been kicked out of the university because of his repeated drunkenness and rowdiness. The young man in *Frühlings Erwachen* has been expelled from school by puritanical authorities for someone else's offense. In *Dr. Mabuse, der Spieler* as well as in *Spione* the central character is clever, complicated, and devious. In both films the roles of the law-enforcement officers who come to terms with the master criminals are strikingly diminished. The hero in *Der Mann ohne Namen* is the "Million Dollar Thief" Peter Voss; at the end of the film, having helped the

[143]

police capture another crook, he disappears and escapes punishment. *Variété* is the story of events that lead a decent man to kill, as is *Alkohol*.

In many cases the hero or heroine of a popular German film becomes an outcast through strange circumstances outside his or her own control. The psychodramatic point is still the same, however: The hero or heroine is a pariah. The hapless Balduin in *Der Student von Prag* becomes a complete social outcast after his mirror image has slain in a duel a man whose life Balduin had promised to spare. In *Madame Du Barry* the title character is portrayed as little more than a common whore who has done well; the same is also true of the heroines of *Anna Boleyn* and *Lady Hamilton*. The subplot in *Die Verrufenen* revolves around the streetwalker Emma, who finally becomes involved in a tawdry burglary. The tragedy of *Die wunderbare Lüge der Nina Petrowna* reduces to the heroine's inability to free herself from the bondage of being the mistress of a wealthy man. More obliquely the same is true of the heroine of *Asphalt*. *Der letzte Mann* portrays the tale of a hotel doorman who becomes an outcast from his petty bourgeois milieu when he is demoted to the job of a men's room attendant. In *Ich hab' mein Herz in Heidelberg verloren* the student Rudolf must give up his love for Klärchen or be expelled from the university. The hero of *Graf Cohn* is a Jew who remains an outcast in spite of having married into the German aristocracy. In *Der Golem, wie er in die Welt kam*, it is the entire Jewish community that is portrayed— not without sympathy on the conscious level—as a pariah.[57]

The criminal or outcast portrayed as the real hero or heroine of a film story is a device hardly ever found in the French popular cinema of the decade. Only three films fall into this category: *Crainquebille*, *Les Misérables*, and *La Nouvelle aurore*. In these three the meaning and emphasis is quite different from what is typical in the German films made in this mode. In Germany the impact of the Versailles Treaty burdened not just the Imperial Regime, which had fallen in 1918. The entire German nation, rather, was saddled with the onus of being guilty for the outbreak of World War I. The guilt clause of the treaty branded Germany a criminal nation. The collective obsession with this accusation of guilt reflected itself in Germany's most popular films, first, in the guilt theme and, second, in the characterization of the criminal or the outcast as hero. During the 1920s many Germans came to feel that the nation was an outcast among nations, a pariah. Germany had had her colonies taken from her. Many nations boycotted German goods. She had been forced to pay reparations to her former enemies, a situation with which no segment of the German population was pleased.[58] Germany's single most significant diplomatic triumph of the 1920s was her success in establishing relationships with the Soviet Union, Europe's other pariah nation. It is interesting that in a number of instances in Weimar popular films a moral ambiguity is expressed about characters. There are figures who are guilty but are not brought to account for their deeds: *Der Mann ohne Namen* and *Metropolis*. There is guilt with extenuating circumstances as in *Die Herrin der Welt, Geschlecht in Fesseln, Variété,* and *Der Student von Prag,* as well as guilt that is only imagined (*Die Buddenbrooks*), and guilt that is based on false accusation (*Frühlings Erwachen*). Sometimes there is a recognition of the guilt and a coming clean of it, and sometimes not. The confusion in the representation of the guilt theme in German popular films likely represents the national situation after World War I—a tortured, confused nonacceptance of the defeat of 1918 wedded to an unwillingness to come to terms with the charges of responsibility and guilt for the war contained in the Versailles Treaty.

Another confused minor theme of the Weimar popular cinema is that of conflict between generations. The weakness and degeneracy of the younger generation is emphasized in a number of films: *Der alte Fritz, Asphalt, Der Bettelstudent, Die Buddenbrooks, Der Golem, wie er in die Welt kam, Fridericus Rex* (1922), *Mutter Krausens Fahrt ins Glück, Die Puppe* (1919), and obliquely in *Der Walzertraum* (1925). In an equal number of the popular films of the 1920s, however, that conflict is portrayed in reverse: The younger generation is presented as being both stronger and more capable than the older generation. This is so in *Alkohol, Der Berg des Schicksals, Die elf Schillschen Offiziere, Frühlings Erwachen, Die Heilige und ihr Narr* (1928), *Der Katzensteg, Metropolis,* and *Die vom Niederrhein.* In several other movies the conflict between generations is represented. But its significance is neutralized in that neither the younger nor the older generation is portrayed as being in the right: *Die Pest in Florenz, Die Verrufenen,* and *Zwei Menschen* (1923).

The contradictory handling of the generation conflict represents a confusion in the cinematographic dream work. Nothing like it is found in the French popular cinema of the same decade. The German films of the 1920s reflect a tortured, unconscious working and reworking of various materials that refer back to the war of 1914–18, the trauma of an unassimilated defeat and the ensuing revolution of 1918/19, and the liabilities that became the legacy of a guilt-plagued and unpopular republic. The generation conflict seems to relate in its several forms to a situation in which the younger generation accomplishes what the older generation failed to achieve without discrediting the older generation. This is often the case. To cite two examples, in *Der Berg des Schicksals* a young man conquers a mountain his father died trying to climb, and at an entirely different dramatic level, in *Metropolis* the son of the city's master Fredersen discovers the secret to social order and class harmony in love. This might seem to reflect the wish that a new regime would have come to power in Germany after World War I, which—without discrediting the heritage of the old regime—would accomplish what the old regime had failed to achieve. Yet this "wish" is not elaborated as such; it is not part of a fantasy of the wish-fulfillment sort. It is rather a crudely articulated thought, fraught with elements of reversal in its actual representation in the films.

Since the miseries that obsessed so many Germans were thought by them to come from a single source—the loss of the war—it might be assumed that many popular Weimar films would have disguised a wish to avenge the defeat of 1918. Although a handful of films from the decade do refer to the revenge motif, revenge itself in these movies is either repressed, frustrated, or leads to disaster for the avenger. Again, no wish is expressed, merely a confused thought.

A final element is, however, somewhat clearer. Suicides are frequent in the popular movies of Weimar Germany.[59] *Frühlings Erwachen, Geschlecht in Fesseln, Graf Cohn,* and *Das indische Grabmal* all treat suicide as a central theme. Count von Toll slits his wrist in *Dr. Mabuse, der Spieler* and Mabuse's employee Cora meekly takes a suicide capsule that is slipped to her. The agent who takes a suicide pill is also part of the plot of *Spione.* In *Mutter Krausens Fahrt ins Glück,* the heroine kills herself and takes a little girl with her "into happiness." In *Die wunderbare Lüge der Nina Petrowna* Nina shoots herself. The parents of Felix in *Prinz Kuckkuck* commit double suicide of an unspecified nature. Balduin's shooting of his mirror image in *Der Student von Prag,* whereby he himself dies, is a displaced form of suicide. In *Die vom Niederrhein* Hans contemplates suicide but is prevented from following through by the intervention of his girl friend. Likewise, Robert Kramer is prevented from jumping off a bridge in *Die Verrufenen* by Emma, who happens by. In *Faust,* the learned protagonist is prevented from drinking poison by Mephisto. Finally, Frederick the Great claims in *Der alte Fritz* that the happiest day of his life will be the one on which he leaves this world.

This obsession with suicide is quantitatively not as important as the other themes in German popular films with which this essay has dealt. The thoughts of self-destruction or the act itself seem to refer to the war of 1914–18 and further back to prewar policy. From 1895 on Wilhelm's Germany had pursued a foreign policy that was "purely adventurous."[60] The irony of unified Germany was that her industrial and economic development had outstripped her political importance in the world.[61] The adventurous policy of the German government in the two decades prior to World War I was intended to rectify that situation.[62] The war itself was from Germany's point of view an attempt to carry out the final stage of rectification. It backfired, turning into the grandest adventure of all: a suicidal campaign fought on two fronts. The ambitious policy, which climaxed in a suicidal war, was a miscalculated and ill-timed "bid for world power" ("Griff nach der Weltmacht"). The awareness of the danger of this adventurous prewar policy and the grand adventure of the war itself are reflected in German popular films of the 1920s at two other levels as well. The "bid for world power" was always recognized as a perilous business.[63] A number of Weimar films represent social climbing as a high risk: *Madame Du Barry, Lady Hamilton, Anna Boleyn, Graf Cohn*, and *Der Student von Prag*. Moreover, the popularity of the unique mountain-climbing film genre with German audiences represents concern with a symbolic perilous adventure of another sort, as in *Der Berg des Schicksals, Der Kampf ums Matterhorn, Die weisse Hölle von Piz Palü*, and *Die Wunder des Schneeschuhs*.

The symbols of Germany's collective obsession with the loss of the war of 1914–18—betrayal, the foreigner as evildoer, guilt, racing against time, dangerous streets, and so forth—are never portrayed in simple one-to-one relationships to the national, collective experience behind them. No one character represents Germany throughout a film, another a betrayer, and so on. The most popular films of

Germany in the 1920s, when analyzed and interpreted, indicate that the nation was inwardly tormented by the national experience of 1914–18, the defeat of 1918, and the revolution, which dragged on into spring of the next year. These elements reflect that the German experience was traumatic rather than simply disturbing, jarring, or disquieting. A careful look at this group of films reveals that a striking number are left unresolved or are sometimes pseudo-resolved with a quick patch-up that dramatically never comes off. The historical experience of a lost war that was not assimilated and a revolution on top of it produced in Germany an unconscious demand for a cinema that was not just thematically, but essentially, different from its French counterpart of the same decade. French films provided release from disquieting national situations through the fairly simple device of fantasies of the wish-fulfillment sort. By contrast, the Weimar German cinema thrashed its difficult, frustrating way through various aspects of the myriad unconscious material of a national trauma, so extensive and complex that it could find no neat cinematographic resolution through wish fantasies.

N O T E S

1. George Huaco, in *Sociology of Film Art* (New York and London: 1965), p. 51, claims that all the expressionist films were popular with the mass audience. The research reflected in this study does not bear that out. Some films, like *Das Kabinett des Dr. Caligaris*, had only limited success in a few urban centers and nowhere else. Others, like *Scherben* and *Schatten*, were seen by so few people that even the urban audience for them was negligible.

2. A. Gheri, "L'Effort allemand," *La Cinématographie française*, no. 81, 22 May 1920, p. 49. H. D., "Conrad Veidt: Student of Prague," *Close-Up*, no. 3, September, 1927, p. 44, develops much the same argument. *Der Film-Kurier*, 6. Jahrg, no. 14, 16 January 1924, p. 1, complained that the German film industry produced no comedies. Six months later the same journal printed an article calling all German film scripts "pathological": *Der Film-Kurier*, 6. Jahrg., no. 149, 26 June

1924, p. 3. Other sources on this point include my unpublished interview with Henri Diamant-Berger and his reflections on the cinema of the 1920s, as well as Louis Chéronet, "Le Cinéma allemand," *Le Crapouillot*, numéro special, "Histoire du cinéma," November 1932, pp. 52, 53.

3. Henri Agel, *Miroir de l'insolite dans le cinéma français* (Paris: 1958), p. 62. Siegfried Kracauer, *From Caligari to Hitler* (Princeton: 1947), p. 107 ff; also, Herbert Ihering, *Von Reinhardt bis Brecht* (Berlin: 1959), II, p. 427; Pierre Leprohon, *Le Cinéma allemand* (Paris: 1928), pp. 12, 13; H. H. Wollenberg, *Fifty Years of German Film* (London: 1948), p. 19; Raymonde Borde, Freddy Buache, and Francis Coutarde, *Le Cinéma realiste allemand* (Lyon: 1965), pp. 10 ff.; "Le Cinéma allemand: la grande époque," *Cinéma 59*, no. 38, July 1959, p. 57.

4. Cheronet, *op. cit.*, p. 53.

5. Kracauer, *op. cit.*, pp. 58–60.

6. Kenneth MacPherson, "As Is," *Close-Up*, no. 1, July 1927, p. 7.

7. Ludwig Kapeller, "Die deutsche Landschaft als Filmbühne," *Die Lichtbildbühne*, Heft 13, 29 March 1919, pp. 30–32; Robert Spa, "Dans les studios de Berlin," *Ciné-Miroir*, 7ème année, no. 147, 27 January 1928, no page number; Paul Rotha, *The Film Till Now* (London: 1962), 2nd impress., pp. 254, 255; Carlos Clarens, *Horror Movies* (London: 1967), p. 43; Kracauer, *op. cit.*, p. 75; Leprohon, *op. cit.*, p. 11.

8. H. A. Potamkin. "Phases of Cinema Unity," *Close-Up*, vol. IV, no. 5, May 1929, p. 33.

9. Rotha, *op. cit.*, pp. 254, 255.

10. Kenneth Macgowan, *Behind the Screen* (New York: 1965), pp. 224, 225; Jean Mitry, *Index historique du cinéma* (Paris:1967), p. 141.

11. Kracuaer, *op. cit.*, p. 105.

12. *Ibid.*, p. 53.

13. MacPherson, *op. cit.*, p. 7.

14. The plot of *Die elf Schillschen Offiziere*, in which "Freikorps" fail to recognize the official end of a war, parallels directly events in Germany after 1918.

15. The name of the town from which the betrayer comes is "Schanden," which is the German plural for "die Schande," which means dishonor, discredit, disgrace, or shame.

16. This conjurs up the so-called "Doppel-Gänger" image that some who have written on Weimar cinema, such as Kracauer, *op. cit.*, Peter Gay, *Weimar Culture* (1969), and Walter Laqueur, *Weimar: A Cultural History* (1974), have cited as exceptionally rich for interpretation. In the truly popular films, however, when the "Doppel-Gänger" motif is present, it seems always to interpret most compellingly as part of the broader theme of betrayal in Weimar cinema.

17. There are, however, a few films in which betrayal does not lead directly to disaster. In these betrayal occurs, but some sort of reasonably pleasant or neutral resolution is still achieved: *Die vom Niederrhein*

(1925); *Ungarische Rhapsodie* (1928); *Die Verrufenen* (1925); *Monna Vanna* (1922).

18. The film also contains another reference to betrayal. Earlier in the film it is discovered that the brother Gründlich has been embezzling funds from the Buddenbrooks' family firm. Thomas calls the accounts that Gründlich has been keeping the books of "a cheat, a betrayer."

19. In the film there is another reference to betrayal. Whymplier had visited the same village before, fallen, and been nursed back to health by Anton's wife Felicitas. Neighbors had planted in Anton's mind the notion that she was having an affair with the Englishman. This turns out to be untrue, and Anton feels ashamed for ever having believed such a tale.

20. For a discussion of German movie's stereotypes of foreign nationalities, see Klaus-Dieter Bärthel, *Die Rolle der Universum Film A.G. bei der ideologischen Beeinflussung der Massen im Sinne der reaktionärsten Kräfte des deutschen Monopolkapitals und ihrer aggressiven Pläne, 1918 bis 1933*, unpublished dissertation, Karl Marx Universität, Leipzig, 1965, pp. 53 ff.

21. On the conscious level this could be interpreted as portraying the conversative viewpoint that upward social mobility is dangerous. Just such an interpretation could certainly be applied, for example, to the plot of *Metropolis*. But, this is problematic. The film was banned during the 1920s in both Italy and Turkey for having Bolshevist tendencies; see Otto Kriegk, *Der deutsche Film in Spiegel der UFA* (Berlin: 1943), pp. 89 ff.

22. Not just the loss of overseas colonies bothered the Germans during the 1920s, as described in Erich Eyck, *A History of the Weimar Republic* (New York: 1970), I, p. 114. For an impression of distaste for the French sending black soldiers to occupy part of the Rheinland after 1918, see Keith Nelson, "The 'Black Horror on the Rhine'; Race as a Factor in Post-WWI Diplomacy," *Journal of Modern History*, 42, 606–28, 1970. Racism in German film-industry circles can be documented from several sources. For example, *Der Kinematograph*, 18. Jahrg., no. 923, 26 October 1924, pp. 13, 14, complained of the distribution of American-made films in India because such films stimulated native disrespect for white women. *Die Deutsche Lichtspiel-Zeitung*, 8. Jahrg., no. 28, 10 July 1920, pp. 7, 8, reported an incident in which Chinese actors, resident in Berlin, were banned from shooting a motion picture in Munich by local police.

23. Kracauer, *op. cit.*, pp. 56, 57. Kracauer misses citing an apt example, *Geheimnisse des Orients*, to support his theory.

24. Eyck, *op. cit.*, p. 39.

25. S. William Halperin, *Germany Tried Democracy* (New York: 1965), pp. 35–49. The most thorough treatment of the treaty itself in English is still found in John W. Wheeler-Bennett, *The Forgotten Peace* (New York: 1939).

26. Halperin, *op. cit.*, p. 50. In fact, the Germans continued advancing in the East even after the very favorable treaty had been concluded.
27. Eyck, *op. cit.*, p. 28.
28. Hans H. Hermann, *Weimar—Bestandsaufnahme einer Republik* (Reinbek bei Hamburg: 1969), p. 77.
29. Eyck, *op. cit.*, p. 138.
30. Halperin, *op. cit.*, p. 93.
31. Ossip K. Flechtheim, *die KPD in der Weimarer Republik* (Frankfurt a.M.: 1966). See also Herman Weber, *Die Wandlung des deutschen Kommunismus* (Frankfurt a.M.: 1969); Otto Winzer, *Revolutionäre Traditionen des Kampfes der deutschen Arbeiterbewegung gegen Militarismus und Krieg* (Berlin: 1956); Alexander Abusch, *Der Irrweg einer Nation: Ein Beitrag zum Verständis deutscher Geschichte* (Berlin: 1960).
32. A. J. Nicholls, *Weimar and the Rise of Hitler* (New York: 1968), p. 14.
33. Andreas Hillgruber, *Deutschlands Rolle in der Vorgeschichte der beiden Weltkriege* (Göttingen: 1967), p. 54.
34. Eyck, *op. cit.*, p. 39. A glimpse of how dependent the Germans were on having the time factor in their favor and meeting their own timetable is found in Barbara Tuchman's *The Guns of August*.
35. Hillgruber, *op. cit.*, p. 57.
36. See Chapter Four, pp. 106–08.
37. In *Dr. Mabuse, der Spieler* a single trickle of blood is seen on Mabuse's hand, in *Faust* a drop of blood when Faustus signs his pact with Mephisto. A bit of blood is seen in *Die weisse Hölle von Piz Palü*, and in *Nosferatu* Harker cuts his finger while slicing bread, which yields a trace of blood.
38. On the surface level only three of Weimar's most popular films deal directly with World War I: *Der Weltkrieg, Unsere Emden,* and *Heimkehr*.
39. Had rational criteria been applied, other candidates for the betrayer of Germany were available. Austria, for example, signed a separate peace with the Allies in 1918. Italy decided in 1915 to enter the war on the side of France and England rather than supporting the Central Powers to which it had been aligned before the war. Or the Americans, for as Erich Eyck, *op. cit.*, p. 126 writes: "Wilson, the 'old Presbyterian,' was linked with the armistice and revolution as another betrayer who gave Germany the stab in the back. . . ." Another nuance on the betrayal theme might have been to have seen England as Germany's natural ally before 1914 and to have felt betrayed by England when she went to war against Germany. The extent to which Germany aspired to a partnership with England is described in Hillgruber, *op. cit.*, pp. 11–13, 18, 19, 26, 30. Oblique references to this hoped-for ally's "infidelity" might be implied in that a number of German films containing the betrayal motif also present the complementary themes of marital infidelity or false alliance (false friendships or deceitful partnerships).

40. Egmont Zechlin, *Die deutsche Politik und die Juden im ersten Weltkrieg* (Göttingen: 1969), pp. 530, 531.
41. *Ibid.*, pp. 522, 523.
42. *Ibid.*, p. 523.
43. *Ibid.*, p. 542. See also H. C. Adler, *Die Juden in Deutschland* (Munich: 1960); Hannah Arendt, *Elemente und Ursprünge totalitarer Herrschaft* (Frankfurt a.M.: 1962); Jocham Bloch, *Judentum in der Krise* (Göttingen: 1966); Karl Thieme, *Judenfeindschaft: Darstellungen und Analysen* (Frankfurt a.M. and Hamburg: 1963). Also, a contemporary source of interest is Adolf Bartels, *Rssse und Volkstum* (Weimar: 1920), 2. Auflage.
44. For a discussion of other, less popular, Weimar films dealing with the street, see Kracauer, *op. cit.*, pp. 157 ff., 252 ff. The theme is also dealt with more briefly in Lotte Eisner, *Die dämonische Leinwand* (Wiesbanden/Biberich: 1955), pp. 126 ff. The most interesting treatment of the street theme is found in Klaus Kreimeier, "Kino als Ideologiefabrik," *Kinemathek*, 9. Jahrg, no. 45, November, 1971.
45. Interestingly, landscapes in German films of the 1920s are usually romanticized or idealized, rather than natural, landscapes. This is particularly clear in the numerous mountaineering films that appealed to Weimar audiences. In these a reversal of the city/street imagery is accomplished: soaring peaks, bright and open stretches of space, and pure, healthy air are represented.
46. Kracauer, *op. cit.*, pp. 49 ff.
47. Huaco, *op. cit.*, p. 45.
48. *Ibid.*, p. 63.
49. Pommer himself pointed out that these historical references were intentionally covered up by the film-makers. I have found no references in contemporary criticism of the 1920s or other literature of the period that pointed to *Mabuse* and *Metropolis* having any possible symbolic relationship to events of the German Revolution of 1918/19.
50. Several other sources on the revolutionary episodes are: Theodore Eschenburg, *Die improvisierte Demokratie* (Munich: 1964); Klaus Epstein, *Matthias Erzberger and the Dilemma of German Democracy* (Princeton: 1959); Erich Matthias, *Zwischen Räten und Gehiemräten: die deutsche Revolutionsregierung, 1918–1919* (Bonn: 1970); Eric Waldman, *The Spartacist Uprising of 1919* (Milwaukee: 1958); Eberhard Kolb, *Die Arbeiterräte in der deutschen Innenpolitik 1918–1919* (Düsseldorf: 1962); Eberhard Kolb and Reinhard Rürup (eds.), *Der Zentralrat der deutschen sozialistischen Republik* (Leiden: 1968). Also the classic Arthur Rosenberg, *Die Entstehung der deutschen Republik* (Berlin: 1930); 2nd ed., pp. 116 ff.
51. Allan Mitchell, *Revolution in Bavaria 1918/1919* (Princeton: 1965), pp. 1–237. Also Hermann, *op. cit.*, p. 35. In addition, see Hans Beyers, *Von Novemberrevolution zur Räterepublik* (Berlin: 1957) and Gerhard Schmolze (ed.), *Revolution and Räterepublik in München* (Düsseldorf: 1969).

[153]

52. Hermann, *op. cit.*, p. 35.
53. Interesting Marxist interpretations of the events of 1918/19, besides Abusch and Winzer (which have already been cited), are: J. S. Drabkin, *Die Novemberrevolution 1918 in Deutschland* (Berlin: 1968); Jürgen Kucznski, *Studien zur Geschichte des deutschen Imperialismus*, (Berlin: 1948–50), I and II; Rudolf Lindau, *Revolutionäre Kämpfe 1918–1919* (Berlin: 1960).
54. *Kölnische Volkszeitung*, no. 954, Morgen Ausgabe, December 4, 1918, p. 1. The comment on Eisner was in an editorial supporting the formation of an independent Rhinish Republic, a cause fostered at the time by Konrad Adenauer.
55. A. J. Ryder, *The German Revolution of 1918* (Cambridge: 1967), p. 170.
56. Hermann Katorowicz, *Gutachten zur Kriegsschuldfrage 1914* (Frankfurt a.M.: 1967), introduction. For a more general treatment of the question in the 1920s, see Stefan T. Possony, *Zur Bewältigung der Kriegsschuldfrage* (Köln and Opladen: 1968).
57. Consciously anti-Semitic films enjoyed no popularity in Weimar Germany. By contrast, the filmic adaptation of Lessing's *Nathan der Weise* enjoyed good runs most places except in Munich. Another film, *Pogrom*, from 1919, aimed at criticizing anti-Semitism in Czarist Russia, and did good business; see *Die Lichtbildbühne*, 12. Jahrg., no. 31, 2 August 1919, p. 37.
58. In *Unsere Emden* the crew of a defeated German U-boat must surrender to the British. They are, however, treated with full respect. Much is made in the film of the fact that their captors allow the Germans to keep their weapons. The wishful parallel to real events was that Germany in general would have liked to be treated in such a way by the Allies after 1918.
59. In the French popular films of the decade there are but three references to suicide. Dick Frendy shoots himself out of shame in *Le Secret du "Lone Star."* An attempted suicide fails in *La Femme nue* and leads to true love rediscovered. An intended suicide by a child is averted and leads to the child's discovery of the true joys in life in *Visage d'enfants*.
60. Hillgruber, *op. cit.*, p. 20.
61. *Ibid.*, pp. 20, 30 ff.
62. *Ibid.*, pp. 20 ff.
63. *Ibid.*, pp. 57ff.

Conclusion

This study has approached the social function of the popular cinema comparatively. It derives its interpretations only through the mass, public dimension of the film experience. In so doing, it does not imply that this is the sole significant aspect of a popular film's relationship to its viewers. The many levels at which films function suggest numerous worthwhile approaches to their interpretation. Analytically and interpretively this study deals with only the *major* themes of the most popular French and German films of the 1920s. The reader who is acquainted with some of these films, or who knows the French and German history of this period well, will recognize that references to the minor elements in these movies that reinforce the general interpretations made here have been omitted.

The analysis and interpretation of film contents found in this study might be termed "Freudian." However, much of what is done analytically in this essay goes well beyond anything ever suggested by Freud about using cultural artifacts as a reflection of the group psyche. Moreover, much of this essay has nothing whatsoever to do with either Freud or psychology; it is history in the traditional mode written about a somewhat unusual subject. That which does have to do with Freud and psychology is carefully delimited. The claim has been made in the introduction that there are striking enough parallels between the film and the dream to warrant the analysis of popular films as a dreamlike reflection of the shared concerns of the audience to which those films appealed. This hypothesis is pursued to its logical conclusion in the interpretive chapters (Chapters Four and Five). No Freudian theory other than the theory of dreams is utilized in this study.

In the text the terms "group mind" and "collective unconscious" have been used. They are catch phrases meant to describe a phenomenon about which little is known. In this essay their meaning is figurative rather than literal, limited rather than all encompassing. "Group mind" refers to concerns, some conscious and others less so, that were shared by large numbers of people who formed the national, mass audience for films in both France and Germany, respectively. World War I was an event both nations shared as nations. During the war itself, certainly, every Frenchman's and every German's sense of sharing a common destiny with his or her conationals was stimulated and, alternatively, exploited. The sense of nation in both countries had a long prehistory. But with World War I the apex of a certain kind of national process was reached, and the era that followed was—in both countries—intensely nationalistic.

The "group mind" refers to received ideas and notions that enjoyed broad conscious or unconscious currency in a particular society at specific time. Such ideas and notions have, of course, been periodically manipulated by governments or other powerful elements within society. They were felt to be spawned in the first instance, however, by shared experiences. The stuff of which myths is made contains points of reference to reality. The formation of the group mind is situational, hence historical. A rise in group consciousness is precipitated by shared experiences, such as a war. The "group mind" has nothing to do with so-called ethnic characteristics. This is demonstrated in the French and German popular films of the 1920s. Those films reflect, respectively, a differentiated collective obsession with particular historical events and their aftermath. They reflect nothing of the "French spirit" or the "German mentality."

Not all individual members of a group, whether it be a nation or a social class within a nation, are fully aware of the group mentality and the extent of their absorption into it. The group process is complex and precise; it can touch on all aspects of human existence and can manifest itself in such specifics as the particular vocabulary of a national language. Not all potential members of the group are actually individuals who share in the group mentality. The integration of any individual into the conscious and unconscious processes of the group mind or, alternatively, an individual's remaining aloof or hostile to the group mind are variables that can go either way in any individual case. In this regard material, social circumstances and personal, psychological conditions interchangeably modify each other.

The popular French films of the 1920s portrayed the major themes of the orphan, the individual abandoned in the world, the hero, the presence of children, blood seen, and were disposed to landscape and seascape cinematography. The German cinema of the same decade produced popular movies presenting the themes of betrayal, the foreigner as evildoer, the street and the city as ugly and dangerous, the outcast as hero, suicide, and the imagery of

[157]

clocks and unseen blood. The themes that are repeatedly developed and elaborated in French popular films are not to be found in their German counterparts. The reverse is true as well. The two societies worked out their special concerns born of the shared experience of World War I in entirely different film themes and film language.

Some readers may note that some of the themes and imagery of these two respective national cinemas seem to have a kind of existence in the national literary and social traditions of the two countries involved. For example, orphans are common in French novels, particularly in the last few decades of the nineteenth century. And there is circumstantial evidence that a distaste for urban life had developed widely in Germany before 1914. This essay does not deny the possible existence of such elements. Indeed, their pre-existence may very well have influenced the particular mode of representation that was adopted unconsciously in the films of the 1920s in both countries to portray collective, societal concerns. It is outside the scope of this study to pursue every possible point of reference for the period being studied back through even its recent history and tradition in France and Germany. Nor is it necessary. It suffices to point out that readers who enjoy a knowledge of the two national traditions are in a position to bring additional and pertinent understanding to bear upon the material presented here. What is most important for the interpretation of films in this context is the awareness that what counts in a popular culture form is the particular mixture of old and new symbols that it employs. Insofar as the respective national cinemas might have drawn on some elements from French and German cultural traditions, what is significant is the selection. The movies, as it were, picked out only certain aspects of the cultural heritage of the nation for exploitation to the mass audience.

This study has not concerned itself with evaluating or criticizing individual films. It is, however, little argued that the German cinema of the 1920s experienced a "Golden Age." Certainly German films were more complex in their plots, more provocative in their thematic material, and more imaginative visually than their French counterparts. Thus, it might be tempting to conclude that a national cinema that appeals to the mass audience of a society that had just gone through a collective trauma—as Germany had in 1918—tends to produce particularly expressive films. On the surface there seems to be supporting evidence for this conclusion in other situations. The Soviet cinema reached its acme in the difficult years of the late 1920s and early 1930s; the American film, some would say, was best during the Depression; Italian Neo-Realism flourished during the troubled decade following World War II; and the American cinema of the late 1960s and early 1970s seems to be improving as the nation's fortunes deteriorate. The general contention that the cinema of a "traumatized" or troubled society is necessarily imaginative and interesting cinema is a hypothesis to which this study may lend some credence. But it lends only flimsy documentation. The hypothesis cannot be accepted as a maxim of film history and is, at best, a possible starting point for further inquiries into a fascinating topic.

Another area for speculation based on the findings of this study also merits caution. That area is the historical, as opposed to the filmic. Some readers may see in the themes that obsessed the French audiences as reflected through the nation's most popular films psychological tendencies that presumably festered and contributed to France's defeat in 1940. In the German films of the 1920s there seem to be even stronger and clearer indications of shared concerns to which only Hitler and the National Socialists eventually gave pointed and satisfactory answers. The repetitive themes of the popular films of Weimar might then seem to give an explanation, inside out as it were, of the shared concerns of the German people at large and the subsequent appeal of Hitler's message to many of those concerns. While there are grounds in both the French and German cases to see a parallel between collective concerns as reflected in the popular cinema of the 1920s and later events, it is beyond the scope of this study to speculate on such matters. Too little is known of the group process in general and, as of yet, of Hitler's relationship to the German group mind or the true collective psychological condition of France on the eve of World War II to support sound interpretive link-ups between movie themes and later events. This study does not want to fall into the errors of one of its predecessors: *From Caligari to Hitler* by Siegfried Kracauer. Kracauer produced an intriguing account of Weimar cinema that read too much out of the films through hindsight. It began with a perception of Hitlerian Germany (unfortunately not a very profound one) and then attempted to tack a number of filmic themes together and find them all pointing to Hitler's ascension to power in 1933. Kracauer's book, provocative as it was and a forerunner in the field, erred by way of mixing weak history with flimsy psychology. The relationship of collective thoughts as expressed in cultural symbols to actual political events is extremely complex. The dreamlike function of the popular cinema reflects concerns about events of the recent past and their aftermath. There is no indication, either documentary or in theory, that the themes in popular films would be necessarily predictive of future developments.

This study means to be modest about its accomplishments and sincere in the wish that it has opened up larger questions than those it has answered. "National" cinema was unique to the 1920s. But it might be hoped that with some reworking the basic model of analysis and interpretation of films presented here could be preserved and applied to the repetitive themes and motifs of other cinemas.

Appendix A

FRENCH FILMS, 1919–29

The following films were documented as having been the most popular native-produced films with French audiences nationwide during the decade following World War I. The term "popular" is being used here in a comparative, or relative, context. Exact attendance figures for individual movies were difficult to locate. The reporting of such figures was not always accurate. The list was compiled primarily by relying upon reports found in issues of the two most important film trade journals in France during the period: Cinématographie française and Le Courrier cinématographique. In almost every instance, reports of popularity were double-checked. In a few cases, secondary literature offered supporting evidence to verify a film's popularity. The precise references by journal and page for each film's popularity are to be found in the original dissertation on which this book is based (Cinema and Society in France and Germany, 1919–1929, Brandeis University doctoral dissertation in Comparative History, February 1974).

So far as possible, the content analyses of these films were based on viewing the films themselves. This was done at the Cinémathèque française or the Cinémathèque Royale de Belgique. For those films for which no extant copy could be located, content analyses were taken from written summaries found in the movie magazine Ciné-Miroir or, in a few cases, from original scenarios preserved in the Library of Idhec (Paris).

FRENCH POPULAR FILMS (1919–29)
In Alphabetical Order

Film Title	Name of the Director(s)	Year in Which the Film Premiered
L'Atlantide	Jacques Feyder	1921
Le Baiser qui tue	Jean Choux	1928
La Bataille	E. E. Violet	1923
Un Chapeau de paille d'Italie	René Clair	1927
Chignole	René Plaissetty	1919
Coeur fidèle	Jean Epstein	1923
Crainquebille	Jacques Feyder	1923
La Dame de monsereau	René Le Somptier	1923
Les Deux gamines	Louis Feuillade	1920
L'Education de prince	Henri Diamant-Berger	1927
Enfant des Halles	René Le Prince	1924
Les Exploits de Mandrin	Henri Fescourt	1924
La Femme nue	Léonce Perret	1926
La Force de sa vie	René Le Prince	1920
Geneviève	Léon Poirier	1923
La Grand épreuve	A. Duges and A. Ryder	1928
L'Homme du large	Marcel l'Herbier	1920
J'Accuse	Abel Gance	1919
Jocelyn	Léon Poirier	1922
Joueur d'échecs	Raymond Bernard	1926

Film Title	Name of the Director(s)	Year in Which the Film Premiered
Koenigsmark	Léonce Perret	1923
La Légende de Soeur Béatrix	Jacques Baroncelli	1923
La Madone des sleepings	Maurice Gleize	1928
Maldone	Jean Gremillion	1928
La Mendiante de Saint-Sulpice	Charles Burguet	1924
La Merveilleuse vie de Jeanne d'Arc	Marco de Gastyn	1929
Le Miracle des loups	Raymond Bernard	1924
Les Misérables	Henri Fescourt	1925
Les Mystères de Paris	Charles Burguet	1922
Napoléon	Abel Gance	1927
La Nouvelle aurore	Gaston Le Roux	1919
Paris	René Hervil	1924
La Passion et la mort de Jeanne d'Arc	Theodore Dreyer	1927
Le Petit café	Raymond Bernard	1919
Rose France	Marcel l'Herbier	1919
La Rue de la Paix	Henri Diamant-Berger	1927
Le Secret du "Lone Star"	Jacques Baroncelli	1920
Le Secret de Polichinelle	René Hervil	1923
Taô	Gaston Ravel	1921
La Terre promise	Henry Roussel	1924
Tire au flanc	Jean Renoir	1927
Les Transatlantiques	Pierre Colombier	1927
Travail	Henri Pouctal	1919
Les Trois mousquetaires	Henri Diamant-Berger	1921
La Valse de l'Adieu	Henry Roussel	1928

French Popular Films (1919–29)—continued

Film Title	Name of the Director(s)	Year in Which the Film Premiered
Verdun, visions d'Histoire	Léon Poirier	1927
Violettes impériales	Henry Roussel	1923
Visages d'enfants	Jacques Feyder	1923

Appendix B

GERMAN FILMS, 1919–29

The German list of most popular films is longer than the equivalent one for France because the German industry was so much more prolific during the 1920s. German annual feature-film production stood around 200 movies per year during the decade following World War I. The list of most popular German films was put together in much the same way as the French list was assembled. The accuracy of the list for the years 1925–29 is particularly good. From 1925 on, the journal Der Film-Kurier printed a survey of the 50 most popular films in the German Reich for each year. For the first half of the decade reports found in Der Kinematograph, Die Lichtbildbühne, and Der Film-Kurier were the basis for establishing a given German-produced film's popularity with the native audience. The specific references for these findings are in the original dissertation manuscript. Films were seen through the auspices of the Deutsche Kinemathek in West Berlin and the State Film Archives of the German Democratic Republic in East Berlin, both of which have excellent holdings of silent

[165]

films and good facilities for viewing them. As with the French films, some content analyses had to be based on printed materials. These were found in a number of different sources, the best collections of which are available at the Deutsches Institut für Filmkunde in Biberich.

GERMAN POPULAR FILMS (1919–29)
In Alphabetical Order

Film Title	Name of the Director(s)	Year in Which the Film Premiered
Alkohol	E. A. Dupont and K. Lind	1919
Der alte Fritz	Gerhard Lamprecht	1927
Andreas Hofer	Hanns Prechtl	1929
Anna Boleyn	Ernst Lubitsch	1920
Asphalt	Joe May	1929
Der Berg des Schicksals	Arnold Fanck	1924
Der Bettelstudent	J. and L. Fleck	1927
Der blinde Passagier	Victor Janson	1922
Die Buddenbrooks	Gerhard Lamprecht	1923
Danton	Dimitri Buchowetski	1922
Die elf Schillschen Offiziere	Rudolf Meinert	1926
Faust	F. W. Murnau	1926
Die Försterchristl	Friedrich Zelnick	1926
Die Frau im Mond	Fritz Lang	1929
Fridericus Rex	Arzen von Czerespy	1922
Frühlings Erwachen	Richard Oswald	1929
Geheimnisse des Orients	Alexander Wolkoff	1928
Geschlecht in Fesseln	William Dieterle	1928
Der Golem, wie er in die Welt kam	Paul Wegener	1920
Graf Cohn	Karl Boese	1923
Die Heilige und ihr narr	William Dieterle	1928
Heimkehr	Joe May	1928

German Popular Films (1919–29)—continued

Film Title	Name of the Director(s)	Year in Which the Film Premiered
Die Herrin der Welt	Joe May	1919
Ich hab' mein Herz in Heidelberg verloren	Arthur Bergen	1926
Das indische Grabmal	Joe May	1921
Der Kampf ums Matterhorn	M. Bonnard and N. Malasomma	1928
Der Katzensteg	Gerhard Lamprecht	1927
Königin Luise	Karl Grune	1927
Kreuzzug des Weibes	Martin Berger	1926
Lady Hamilton	Richard Oswald	1921
Dr. Mabuse, der Spieler	Fritz Lang	1922
Madame DuBarry	Ernst Lubitsch	1919
Mädchenhandel	Japp Speyer	1926
Der Mann ohne Namen	George Jacoby	1921
Metropolis	Fritz Lang	1927
Monna Vanna	Richard Eichberg	1922
Der Müde Tod	Fritz Lang	1920
Mutter Krausens Fahrt ins Glück	Piel Jutzi	1929
Die Nibelungen	Fritz Lang	1924
Die vom Niederrhein	Walter-Fein	1925
Nosferatu	F. W. Murnau	1921
Die Pest in Florenz	Otto Ripert	1919
Die Puppe	Ernst Lubitsch	1919
Prinz Kuckkuck	Paul Leni	1919
Rivalen	Harry Piel	1923
Spione	Fritz Lang	1928
Der Student von Prag	Henrik Galeen	1926
Das Tanzende Wien	Friedrich Zelnick	1927
Ungarische Rhapsodie	Hanns Schwarz	1928
Unsere Emden	Louis Ralph	1926
Varieté	E. A. Dupont	1925
Die Verrufenen	Gehard Lamprecht	1925
Der Walzertraum	Ludwig Berger	1925
Waterloo	Karl Grune	1929

German Popular Films (1919–29)—continued

Film Title	Name of the Director(s)	Year in Which the Film Premiered
Die Wege zur Kraft und Schönheit	Wilhelm Prager	1925
Die Weisse Hölle von Piz Palü	Arnold Fanck and G. W. Pabst	1929
Der Weltkrieg	Leo Lasko	1927
Wettlauf ums Glück	Bruno Ziener	1923
Wolga-Wolga	Victor Tourjansky	1928
Die Wunder des Schneeschuhs	Arnold Fanck	1920
Die Wunderbare Lüge der Nina Petrowna	Hanns Schwarz	1929
Zwei Menschen	Hanns Schwarz	1923

Bibliography of Selected Items

ORIGINAL SOURCES

Official Documents

Official documents have been used only for topics in the history of the cinema in Germany. In France there are few documents available; those that are have been thoroughly researched by Paul Leglise, *Histoire de la politique du cinéma français: Le Cinéma et la IIIème république*, a work that is cited frequently in this study. The financial records and business correspondence of the Universum Film A.G. from the 1920s were obtained by the Bundesarchiv Koblenz after UFA went bankrupt in the 1950s and the firm was liquidated. These documents evidently came into the possession of the Bundesarchiv because UFA was directly subsidized by the regime during the early years of the Weimar Republic. Normally, the business documents of a private-film-producing firm would not be found in governmental archives.

[169]

Records and correspondence of the German Ministry of the Interior, "Sackgruppe Presse," for the years 1919 to 1929. Folio 1-298, R 431/2497, R 431/2499; Folio 1-287, R 431/2498 (Bundesarchiv Koblenz). These folios contain letters, official communications, and other documents of the German Ministry of the Interior on matters pertaining to film, radio, and the press.

Records and correspondence of the Universum Film A.G. (UFA) package numbered R 109. (Bundesarchiv Koblenz). These are records of the business operations of UFA during the 1920s. The collection is varied, consisting mainly of correspondence, financial reports, and pamphlets prepared by or for UFA.

Personal Sources

Interview with Lotte Eisner (film critic in Germany during the 1920s and historian of the Weimar cinema) in Paris, 9 January 1971.

Interview with Henri Diamant-Berger (French film actor, director, and producer during the 1920s and 1930s) in Paris, 15 April 1971.

Interview with Klaus Kreimeier (sociologist and historian of the German cinema) in Berlin-West, 21 November 1971.

Letter, Dr. Arnold Fanck (German film director and producer during the 1920s) to Klaus Kreimeier, 24 April 1972, courtesy of the Deutsche Kinemathek, Berlin-West.

Letter, Gerhard Lamprecht (film director in Weimar Germany and historian of the German silent cinema) to Paul Monaco, 7 May 1972.

Newspapers

Newspapers are not the best of sources for a study of the French and German silent cinema. One Parisian daily, *Bonsoir*, did publish interesting commentaries on the contemporary situation in cinema, particularly from 1920 to 1925 when the outspoken Auguste Nardy was responsible for the weekly column on the movies. The right-wing *L'Action française* printed a number of articles on various matters involving the government and film industry in France. Otherwise, the daily press of the 1920s in both France and Germany was scanned with the intention of establishing an overview of the sort of advertising that was placed by movie theaters and film producers for particular films and to establish the general tenor of movie criticism in the daily press during the 1920s.

L'Action française (Paris), selected numbers for the years 1919–29.

L'Ami du Peuple (Paris), selected numbers for the years 1919–29.

Berliner Morgenpost (Berlin), selected numbers for the years 1919–29.

Berliner Tagesblatt (Berlin), selected numbers for the years 1919–29.

Bonsoir (Paris), selected numbers for the years 1919–29.

Figaro (Paris), selected numbers for the years 1919–29.

L'Intansigeant (Paris), selected numbers for the years 1926–29.

Kölnische Volkszeitung (Cologne), several numbers from the year 1918.

La Matin (Paris), selected numbers for the years 1919–29.

Le Populaire (Paris), selected numbers from the years 1919–29.

Quotidien (Paris), selected numbers for the years 1923–27.

Vossische Zeitung (Berlin), selected numbers for the years 1924–28.

Magazines and Journals

French and German film trade journals and movie magazines provide a broad range of original materials on the film industry of the era in general and on particular films as well. Although they have been used but rarely by scholars, they are a vital source of information and contemporary opinion about the cinema, a reflection of the mentality of the people working in movie-making in both countries, and a unique repository of insight and comment on all matters cinematographic. Their use is a must for anyone who would study the cinemas of these two countries seriously. Material from them has been used and cited for almost every section of this study. They are particularly significant as a source of information about how the film industry actually functioned in France and Germany during the 1920s, for their reporting on a given film's box-office success or lack of it, and, in some cases, for providing capsule summaries of a given film that itself is no longer accessible to researchers. Most articles published in these journals and magazines during the 1920s were unsigned. Of those that were signed, most were simple reports rather than being editorial or philosophical in nature. Hence, they have not been cited as single items in this bibliography. Sometimes, however, the reader will notice that the notes do refer to articles or reports from these journals and magazines under the name of the person actually responsible for the piece.

Allgemeine Kino-Börse, 1919, 1920, 1921.
Bulletin Internationale du Cinèmatographie, 1930, 1931.
Cinéa-Ciné pour tous, 1921, 1922, 1923, 1924.
Le Cinéma et l'écho du cinéma réunis, 1920, 1921.
La Cinématographie française, 1918–29.
Cinéma-Spectacles, 1928.
Ciné-Miroir, 1921–29.
Cinémonde, 1928, 1929.
Close-Up, 1927, 1928, 1929, 1930; published in English in Switzerland.
Le Courrier Cinématographique, 1918–29.
Deutsche Lichtspiel-Zeitung (Berlin) 1920, 1921.
Internationale Filmschau, 1919–22.
Der Film-Kurier, 1919–30.
Die Illustrierte Film Woche, 1921, 1922.
Der Illustrierte Film-Kurier, 1920–29.
Hebdo-Film, 1923–26.
Der Kinematograph, 1918–28.
Die Lichtbildbühne, 1919–29.
Lichtbildbühne Tagesdienst, 1922, 1923.
MKB Film Rundschau, 1928.
Münchener Film-Kurier, 1921.
Neue Illustrierte Film Woche, 1923, 1924.
Paimann's Filmlisten, 1922, 1923, 1924.
La Petite Illustration, 1922–29.
Das Reichsfilmblatt, 1922, 1923.
La Revue du cinéma, 1929, 1930, 1931.

Films

Numerous films produced in France and Germany during the 1920's have been viewed. Those movies have served as original sources for this study. The most popular films are catalogued in Appendix A (for France) and Appendix B (for Germany).

SECONDARY SOURCES

Cinema History

Agel, Henri, "La France et le cinéma français," *Chronique Sociale de France*, 62ème année, no. 4/5, July/October 1954, pp. 352–7.
——, *Miroirs de l'insolite dans le cinéma français*, Paris, 1958.

Bardech, Maurice and Brasillach, Robert, *Histoire du cinéma*, 2 vols., Paris, 1964.
Bärthel, Klaus-Dieter, *Die Rolle der Universum-Film A.G. bei der ideologischen Beeinflussung der Massen im Sinne der reaktionärsten Kräfte des deutschen Monopolkapitals und ihrer aggressiven Pläne 1918 bis 1933*, unpublished dissertation, Karl Marx Universität, Leipzig, 1965.
Boll, André, *Le Cinéma et son histoire*, Paris, 1941.
Borde, Raymonde, Buache, Freddy, and Coutarde, Francis, *Le Cinéma réaliste allemand*, Lyon, 1965.
Brownlow, Kevin, *The Parade's Gone By*, London, 1969.
Brunius, Jacques, *En Marge du cinéma français*, Paris, 1954.
Bucher, Felix, *Screen Series: Germany*, New York and London, 1970.
Buchner, Hans, *Im Banne des Films*, Munich, 1927.
Canudo, Ricardo, *L'Usine aux images*, Geneva, 1927.
Cervoni, Albert, "Le Cinéma social," *La Cinématographie française*, Mensuel 4, April 1964, no page numbers.
Chéronet, Louis, "Le Cinéma allemand," *Le Crapouillot*, numéro spéciale, November 1932, pp. 51–54.
Chevanne, André, *L'Industrie du cinéma*, Bordeaux, 1933.
Clarens, Carlos, *Horror Movies*, London, 1967.
Coissac, G.-Michel, *Histoire du cinématographe*, Paris, 1925.
Dadek, Walter, *Die Filmwirtschaft*, Freiburg, 1957.
Dietrich, Valeska, *Alfred Hugenberg: Ein Manager in der Publizistik*, unpublished dissertation, Freie Universität, Berlin-West, 1960.
Domarchi, Jean, "Murnau," in *Anthologie du cinéma*, Paris, 1966, I, pp. 333–84.
Duché, Jean, "La Peinture et les peintres dans le cinéma," *Formes et Couleurs*, 8ème année, no. 61, 1946, no page numbers.

Eisner, Lotte, "Comment écrire l'histoire du cinéma, *Postif*, no. 6, October 1952, pp. 37–40.

———, *Dämonische Leinwand*, Wiesbaden/Biberich, 1955.

———, *F. W. Murnau*, Paris, 1964.

———, "Notes sur quelques films allemands," *Cahiers du cinéma*, Tome XV, no. 90, December 1958, pp. 18, 19.

Felix, Jean, *Le Chemin du cinéma*, Paris, 1934.

Fescourt, Henri et al, *Le Cinéma des origines à nos jours*, Paris, 1932.

———, "Esprit moderne," *Schémas*, February 1927, pp. 33–41.

Ford, Charles, *Bréviaire du cinéma*, Paris, 1945.

Freschi, Jean-André, "Feuillade, l'homme aimanté," *Cahiers du cinéma*, no. 160, November 1964, pp. 31–39.

Gaumont Films, *Notice sur les établissements*, pamphlet printed by the firm, Paris, no date.

Gregor, Joseph, *Das Zeitalter des Films*, Vienna and Leipzig, 1932.

Haage, Hans, *Das gab's nur zweimal*, Berlin, 1959.

Hauser, Arnold, *The Social History of Art*, New York, 1962, IV.

Huaco, George, *The Sociology of Film Art*, New York and London, 1965.

Ihering, Herbert, *Von Reinhardt bis Brecht*, Berlin, 1959, II.

Jason, Alexander, *Der Film in Ziffern und Zahlen*, Berlin, 1925.

———, *Handbuch der Filmwirtschaft*, Berlin, 1930, 3 vols.

———, *Jahrbuch der Filmindustrie*, Berlin, 1923, I.

———, *Jahrbuch der Filmindustrie*, Berlin, 1926, II.

Jeanne, René, *Cinéma 1900*, Paris, 1965.

Jeanne, René and Ford, Charles, *Le Cinéma et la presse*, Paris, 1961.

———, *Histoire illustrée du cinéma*, Verviers, 1966, I.

———, *Histoire encyclopédique du cinéma*, Paris, 1947, I.

Kalbus, Oskar, *Vom Werden deutscher Filmkunst*, Altona/Bahrenfeld, 1935.

Knight, Arthur, *The Livliest Art*, New York, 1957.

Kracauer, Siegfried, "Films de guerre et films militaires allemands," *Le Revue du cinéma*, 3ème année, no. 22, 1 May 1931, pp. 32–37.

———, *From Caligari to Hitler*, Princeton, 1947.

Kreimeier, Klaus, "Das Kino als Ideologiefabrik," *Kinemathek*, 9. Jahrg., no. 45, November 1971.

Kriegk, Otto, *Der deutsche Film im Spiegel der UFA*, Berlin, 1943.

Lamprecht, Gerhard, *Deutsche Stummfilme*, Berlin, 1965–71, 8 vols.

Leglise, Paul, *Histoire de la politique du cinéma français: Le Cinéma et la IIIème république*, Paris, 1970.

Leprohon, Pierre, *L'Exotisme et le cinéma*, Paris, 1945.

———, *Le Cinéma allemand*, Lille, 1928.

———, *Cinquantes ans de cinéma*, Paris, 1954.

———, *Jean Epstein*, Paris, 1964.

———, *Le Monde du cinéma*, Paris, 1967.

Lewis, Howard, *The Motion Picture Industry*, New York, 1933.

Manvell, Roger and Fraenkel, Heinrich, *The German Cinema*, London, 1971.

Manz, H. P., *UFA und der frühe deutsche Film*, Zurich, 1963.

Mercillon, Henri, *Cinéma et monopoles*, Paris, 1953.

Mitry, Jean, *Histoire du cinéma*, Paris, 1969, 2 vols.

Moussinac, Léon, *L'Age Ingrat du cinéma*, Paris, 1967.

No author, "Si Charles Pathé nous etait conté," *Cinémonde*, no. 1182, 4 April 1957, pp. 22, 23.

Oertel, Rudolf, *Filmspiegel*, Vienna, 1941.

Olimsky, Fritz, *Tendenzen der Filmwirtschaft und deren Auswirkung auf die Filmpresse*, unpublished dissertation, Friedrich Wilhelm Universität, Berlin, 1931.

Quinn, James, *The Film and Television as an Aspect of European Culture*, Leyden, 1968.

Regierung und Film, pamphlet, Privatdruck, Berlin, 1919

Riess, Curt, *Das gab's nur einmal*, Hamburg, 1956.

Rotha, Paul, *The Film Till Now*, Feltham-Middlesex, 1962.

Sadoul, Georges, *Histoire du cinéma français*, Paris, 1962.

———, *Histoire d'un art: Le Cinéma des origines à nos jours*, Paris, 1949.

Sichier, Jacques, "Dans le cinéma français l'aventure ne dépasse pas le coin de la rue," *L'Écran*, January 1958, pp. 10–17.

Toeplitz, Jerzy, *Geschichte des Films*, Berlin, 1972, 2 vols.

Traub, Hans, *Die Ufa*, pamphlet, Berlin, 1943.

Vincent, Carl, *Histoire de l'art cinématographique*, Brussels, no date, 2nd ed.

Wahl, Lucien, "Films de guerre français," *La Revue du cinéma*, 3ème année, no. 22, 1 May 1931, pp. 21–25.

Wesse, Curt, *Grossmacht Film*, Berlin, 1928.

Wolffsohn, Karl, *Jahrbuch der Filmindustrie*, Berlin, 1930, IV.

Wollenberg, H. H., *Fifty Years of German Film*, London, 1948.

Zgliniki, Friedrich, *Der Weg des deutschen Films*, Frankfurt am Main, 1955.

Film Theory

The most expansive literature on film theory is in the French language. French film theorists have generally emphasized the aesthetic aspects of the cinema rather than the sociological and historical. The *Revue Internationale de Filmologie* devoted numerous pages, particularly during the late 1940s and early 1950s, to articles on the physiopsychological effects of film viewing. These issues of the *Revue* provide intriguing insights into the filmic experience. Anyone interested in cinema viewed from a historical perspective will want to read Peter Bächlin's *Der Film als Ware*, first published in 1945, reprinted in paperback version in Spring 1973. The soundest monograph in English is I. C. Jarvie's *Towards A Sociology of Cinema* (1970). Two books by Parker Tyler, *Magic and Myth of The Movies* (1947) and *Three Faces of The Film* (1967), provide interesting notions about the interaction of movies, their makers, and their audiences; unfortunately, in both works the accounts are rambling and uneven, and the prose is often pretentious and irritating. The author is well-acquainted with the recent books presenting a semiological approach to film. Since they and the theories of film they develop were of no direct use to this study, they are not included here.

Agel, Henri, "Le Cinéma et le vertige de la surrealité," *Études cinématographiques*, vol. 2, no. 8, Spring 1961, pp. 65–72.

Altenloh, Emelie, *Zur Soziologie des Kinos*, Jena, 1914.

Arnheim, Rudolf, *Film als Kunst*, Berlin, 1932.

Arnoux, Alexandre, "Mise au point," *Revue Fédéralist*, 10éme année, cahier 103, November 1927, pp. 6–10.

Ayfre, Amedée, *Le Cinéma et sa vérité*, Paris, 1969.

Bach-Tesseyre, Michele, *Étude Critique sur la communication cinématographique*, typescript essay, 1964, in the collections of the library Idhec, Paris.

Bächlin, Peter, *Der Film als Ware*, Basel, 1945.

Bagier, Guido, *Der kommende Film*, Berlin, Stuttgart, and Leipzig, 1928.

Balazs, Bela, *Der sichtbare Mensch, eine Film-Dramaturgie*, Halle, no date, 2nd ed.

Bataille, R., "Le Rêve et le cinéma," *Ciné-Amateur*, no. 257, December 1960, pp. 4–9.

Becker, Raymond de, "Pour une psychanalyse du cinéma," *La Table Ronde*, no. 109, January 1957, pp. 79–89.

Benjamin, Walter, *Das Kunstwerk im Zeitalter seiner technischen Reproduzierbarkeit*, Frankfurt am Main, 1955.

Bideau, Henriette, "Le Cinéma et les mythes," *Triades*, Tome IX, no. 3, Autumn 1961, pp. 50–59.

Bonnefoy, Claude, *Le Cinéma et ses mythes*, Paris, 1965.

Bourgeois, Jacques, "Rêve et cinéma," *Arts et Lettres*, no. 11, 1948, pp. 86–93.

Braun-Larrieu, André, *Le Rôle social du cinéma*, Paris, 1938.

Bunuel, Luis, "A Statement," *Film Culture*, no. 21, Summer 1960, pp. 41, 42.

Chevally, Freddy, "Vie du film et vie réele," *Close-Up*, vol. 1, no. 2, January 1928, pp. 72–77.

Cohen-Seat, Gilbert, *Essai sur les principes d'une philosophie du cinéma*, Paris, 1958.

Cohen-Seat, G., Gestaut, H., and Bert, J., "Modification de l'E.E.G. pendant la projection cinématographique," *Revue Internationale de Filmologie*, Tome V, no. 16, January/March 1954, pp. 7–64.

Consiglio, A., "La Fonction sociale du cinéma," *Revue Internationale du Cinéma Éducateur*, Véme année, no. 11, November 1933, pp. 755–62.

Davay, M. P., "Mythe et cinéma," *Le Cinéma fait social*, XXVII éme semaine sociale universitaire, 20–25 April, 1959, Brussells, pp. 99–125.

Deprun, Jean, "Cinéma et transfert," *Revue Internationale de Filmologie*, no. 2., September/October 1927, pp. 295–07.

Desoille, Robert, "Le Rêve éveillé et la filmologie," *Revue Internationale de Filmologie*, no. 2, September/October 1947, pp. 197–203.

Doat, Jan, *Entrée du public*, Paris, 1947.

Durand, Jacques, *Le Cinéma et son public*, Paris, 1958.

———, "Le Film est-il une marchandise?" *Le Cinéma fait social*, XXVIIéme semaine sociale universitaire, 20–25 April, 1959, Brussels, pp. 30–47.

Epstein, Jean, *L'Intelligence d'une machine*, Paris, 1946.

Fauré, Elie, *Fonction du cinéma*, Geneva, 1964.

Feldman, Erich, *Theorie der Massenmedien*, Munich and Basel, 1962.

Filloux, Jean-Claude, *Questions de psychologie sociale*, Paris, 1963.

Fulchignoni, Enrico, *La Civilisation de l'image*, Paris, 1969.

————, "Examen d'un test filmique," *Revue Internationale de Filmologie*, Tome II, no. 6., no date, pp. 173–84.

Fülöp-Miller, René, *Die Phantasiemaschine*, Berlin, 1931.

Galfriet, R. and Segal, J., "Cinéma et physiologie des sensations," *Revue Internationale de Filmologie*, no. 3/4, October 1948, pp. 289–93.

Gestaut, Henri and Roger, Annette, "Effets psychologiques, somatiques, et électroencéphalographiques du stimulus luminex intermittent rhythmiques," *Revue Internationale de Filmographie*, II, no. 7/8, 1948, pp. 215–31.

Gemelli, Agostino, "Le Film, procédé d'analyse projective," *Revue Internationale de Filmologie*, Tome II, no. 6, 1948, pp. 135–9.

Gessner, Robert, *The Moving Image*, New York, 1968.

Godmé, J. P., "Philosophie du cinéma," *Revue Fédéraliste*, 10ème année, cahier 103, November 1927, pp. 86–93.

Guicharnaud, Jacques, "L'Univers magique et l'image cinématographique," *Revue Internationale de Filmologie*, no. 1, July/August 1947, pp. 39–42.

Gusdorf, Georges, "Reflexions sur la civilisation de l'image," *Rechercheset Débats*, cahier 33, 4ème trimestre, 1960, pp. 11–37.

Harms, Rudolf, *Philosophie des Films*, Leipzig, 1926.

Heimann, Paul, "Der Film als Ausdruck der Gegenwarts Kultur," *Universitas*, 12. Jahrg., Heft 4, 1957, pp. 345–54.

Huss, Roy and Silverstein, Norman, *The Film Experience*, New York, Evanston, and London, 1968.

Huyghe, René, *Dialogue avec le visible*, Paris, 1961.

Idhec, Cours et conférences, typescript copy of the session of 27 February 1945, "Le Cinéma devant la société," library of Idhec, Paris.

Jarvie, I. C., *Towards A Sociology of Cinema*, London, 1970.

Landry, Lionel, "La Propaganda par le film," *Cinéa-Ciné pour tous*, série no. 6, 1 February 1924, pp. 6–8.

Lelord, G., "Film et psychophysiologie," *Revue Internationale de Filmologie*, Tome XI, no. 36/37, January–June 1961, pp. 3–14.

Leiriens, Jean, *Vues dur le cinéma*, Brussels, 1947.

Lindgren, Ernest, *The Art of the Film*, London, 1948.

Macgowan, Kenneth, *Behind The Screen*, New York, 1965.

Malraux, André, "Esquisse d'une psychologie du cinéma," *Formes et Couleurs*, 8ème année, no. 6, 1946, pp. 5–8.

Mandion, René, *Cinéma, Reflet du monde*, Paris, 1944.

Mauriac, Claude, *L'Amour du cinéma*, Paris, 1954.

Maurois, André, "La Poésie du cinéma," *L'Art cinémato-graphique*, III, 1927, p. 5.

Mayer, J. P., *Sociology of Film*, London, 1948.

McLuhan, Marshall, *Understanding Media*, London, 1966.

Mead, Margaret, "Why We Go To The Movies," *Redbook Magazine*, March 1971, pp. 48–52.

Metz, Christian, "À propos de l'impression de realité au cinéma," *Cahiers du cinéma*, nos. 166/167, May/June 1965, pp. 74–82.

Micha, M. R., "Le Cinéma au regard des autres arts," *Le Cinéma fait social*, XXVIIème semaine sociale universitaire, 20–25 April 1959, Brussels, pp. 95–98.

Michotte, A., "Le caractère de 'realité' des projections cinémato-graphiques," *Revue Internationale du Cinéma*, Tome I, no. 3/4, October 1948, pp. 249–62.

Mitry, Jean, *Esthétique et psychologie du cinéma*, Paris, 1963, 1.

Morin, Edgar, *Le Cinéma ou l'homme imaginaire*, Paris, 1956.

————, "Recherches sur le public cinématographique," *Revue Internationale de Filmologie*, Tome IV, no. 12, January-March 1953, no page numbers.

Moussinac, Léon, "Bela Balazs, théoricien du cinéma," *Revue Internationale de Filmologie*, Tome II, no. 6, pp. 195–7.

Musatti, L., "Le Cinéma et la psychanalyse," *Revue Internationale de Filmologie*, Tome II, no. 6, pp. 184–94.

No author, "Écrits psychanalytiques sur le cinéma," *Travail au Film*, no. 1, January 1970, pp. 12–15.

No author, "L'Écran bi-face un oeil derrière la tête: Entretien avec André Green," *Travail au Film*, no. 1, January 1970, pp. 15–22.

No author, "Le Cinéma c'est déjà l'inconscient: Entretien avec Janine Chasseguet-Smirguel," *Travail au Film*, no. 1, January 1970, pp. 23–28.

No author, "Freud et le cinéma," *Travail au Film*, no. 1, January 1970, pp. 2–4.

Oldfield, R. C., "La Perception visuelle des images du cinéma, de la télévision et du radar," *Revue Internationale de Filmologie*, Tome I, no. 3/4, October 1948, pp. 263–80.

Otmar, Karl Freiherr von Aretin, "Der Film als zeitgeschichtliche Quelle," *Politische Studien*, 9. Jahrg., Heft 96, April 1958, pp. 254–68.

Ponzo, Mario, "Cinéma et psychologie," *Revue Internationale de Filmologie*, Tome I, no. 3/4, October 1948, pp. 295–7.

————, "Le Cinéma et les images collectives," *Revue Internationale de Filmologie*, Tome II, no. 6, 1948, pp. 141–52.

Pornon, Charles, *Le Rêve et le fantastique dans le cinéma français*, Paris, 1959.

Potamkin, H. A., "Phases of Cinema Unity," *Close-Up*, vol. IV, no. 5, May 1929, pp. 27–38.

Prokop, Dieter, *Soziologie des Films*, Neuwied and Berlin, 1970.

Radtke, Michael, "Irrwitzige Schlachten: Ein Film Anti-Krieg ist kein Film Anti-Krieg," *Film und Fernsehen*, 9. Jahrg., Heft 5, May 1971, pp. 15–19.

Ramain, Paul, "De l'incohérence onirique à la cohérence cinematographique," *Schémas*, February 1927, pp. 60–67.

Rapport Général des secondes rencontres internationales du film pour la jeuness, Cannes, 20 June–4 July 1961, typescript copy in the library Idhec, Paris.

Sadoul, Georges, "À la recherche de quelques fils conducteurs," *Le Point*, 12ème année, LIX, 1962, pp. 5–13.

Samuels, Charles Thomas, *A Casebook on Film*, New York, 1970.

Soriano, Marc, "Lire, Assister," *Revue Internationale de Filmologie*, Tome 1, no. 3/4, October 1948, pp. 209–304.

Spottiswoode, Raymond, *A Grammar of The Film*, Berkeley and Los Angeles, 1965.

Stepun, Fedor, *Theater und Kino*, Berlin, 1932.

Talbot, Daniel, *Film: An Anthology*, Berkeley and Los Angeles, 1967.

Traub, Hans, *Der Film als politisches Machtmittel*, Munich, 1933.

Treveen, Fritz, "Der Film als Historisches Dokument," *Vierteljahrshefte für Zeitgeschichte*, 3. Jahrg., Heft 1, January 1955, pp. 57–66.

Tyler, Parker, *Magic and Myth of The Movies*, New York, 1947.

——, *Three Faces of the Film*, New York, 1967.

Warshow, Robert, *The Immediate Experience*, Garden City, 1962.

Whitaker, Rod, *The Language of Film*, Englewood Cliffs. 1970.

Witte, Karsten, *Theorie des Kinos; Ideologiekritik der Traumfabrik*, Frankfurt am Main, 1972.

Wolfenstein, Martha and Leites, Nathan, *Movies: A Psychological Study*, Glencoe, 1950.

Yanez, José Echeverria, "Virtualités du cinéma," *Revue Internationale du Cinéma*, Tome II, no. 6, pp. 199–205.

Zazzo, Bianka and René, "Une Expérience sur le comprehension du film," *Revue Internationale de Filmologie*, Tome II, no. 6, pp. 159–61.

Psychology

Diamond, Edwin, *The Science of Dreams*, Garḻen City, 1962.
Foulkes, David, *The Psychology of Sleep*, New York, 1966.
Freud, Sigmund, *The Interpretation of Dreams*, New York, 1965; trans. and ed. by James Strachey.
——, *Massenpsychologie und Ich-Analyse*, Vienna, 1921.
Geiger, Theodor, *Die Masse und ihre Action*, Stuttgart, 1967.
LeBon, Gustav, *La Psychologie des foules*, Paris, 1921.
Lowy, Samuel, *Man and His Fellowman*, London, 1944.
Levi-Strauss, Claude, *Le Cru et le cuit*, Paris, 1964.
——, *La Pensée sauvage*, Paris, 1962.
——, *Les Structures élémentaires de la parenté*, Paris, 1947.
——, *Totemism*, Middlesex, 1969; trans. by Rodney Needham.
Rank, Otto, *The Myth of The Birth of the Hero*, New York, 1964.
Webb, Wilse B., *Sleep: an Experimental Approach*, New York, 1968.
Witkin, Herman A. and Lewis, Helen B. (eds.), *Experimental Studies of Dreaming*, New York, 1967.

French and German History

FRANCE

Armengaud, André, *Histoire des populations françaises et leurs attitudes devant la vie depuis le 18ème siècle*, Paris, 1948.
——, *La Population française au XXème siècle*, Paris, 1965.
Beaujeu-Garnier, Jacqueline, *La Population française*, Paris, 1969.
Brenier, Henri, *French Points of View*, Marseille, 1921; trans. by the author.
Chastenet, Jacques, *Les Années d'illusions, 1918–1931*, Paris, 1960.
Clemenceau, Georges, *Grandeurs et misères d'une victoire*, Paris, 1930.
Ebray, Alcide, *A Frenchman Looks at The Peace*, New York, 1927; trans. by E. W. Dickes.
Gautier, Charles, *L'Angleterre et nous*, Paris, 1922.
Huber, Michel, Bunlé, Henri, and Boverat, Fernand, *La Population de la France. Son Évolution et ses perspectives*, Paris, 1950.
Hughes, Judith M., *To the Maginot Line*, Cambridge, 1971.

Köller, H. and Töpfer, B., *Frankreich, ein historisches Abriss,* Berlin, 1969, II.

L'Hullier, Fernand, *De la Sainte-Alliance au pacte atlantique,* Neuchatel, 1955, 4 vols.

Lederer, Ivo J., *The Versailles Settlement,* Boston, 1960.

Mayer, Arno P., *Politics and Diplomacy of Peacemaking: Containment and Counterrevolution at Versailles 1918–1919,* New York, 1969.

Mantoux, Paul, *Les Délibérations du Conseil du Quatre (24 mars–28 juin 1919; notes de l'officier interprète,* Paris, 1955, II.

Nadeau, Ludovic, *La France se regarde: Le Problème de la natalité,* Paris, 1931.

Potjomkin, W. J., *Geschichte der Diplomatie,* Berlin, 1948, 3.

Petrie, Charles, *Diplomatic History,* London, 1948.

Renouvin, Pierre, *Histoire des relations internationales,* "Les Crises du XXème siècle," I, Paris, 1957.

Schuman, Frederick L., *War and Diplomacy in the French Republic,* New York and London, 1931.

GERMANY

Abusch, Alexander, *Der Irrweg einer Nation: Ein Beitrag zum Verständnis deutscher Geschichte,* Berlin, 1960.

Adler, H. C., *Die Juden in Deutschland,* Munich, 1960.

Arendt, Hannah, *Elemente und Ursprünge totalitarer Herrschaft,* Frankfurt am Main, 1962.

Beyers, Hans, *Von der Novemberrevolution zur Räterrepublik,* Berlin, 1957.

Bloch, Jocham, *Judentum in der Krise,* Göttingen, 1966.

Chambers, *The War Behind the War, 1914–1918,* London, 1939.

Dederke, Karlheinz, *Reich und Republik,* Stuttgart, 1969.

Drabkin, J. S., *Die November Revolution 1918 in Deutschland,* Berlin, 1968.

Epstein, Klaus, *Matthias Erzberger and the Dilemma of German Democracy,* Princeton, 1959.

Eschenberg, Theodore, *Die improvisierte Demokratie,* Munich, 1969.

Eyck, Erich, *A History of the Weimar Republic,* New York, 1970, 2 vols.

Flechtheim, Ossip K., *Die KPD in der Weimarer Republik,* Frankfurt am Main, 1966.

Gay, Peter, *Weimar Culture,* New York, 1969.

[182]

Halperin, S. William, *Germany Tried Democracy*, New York, 1965.

Hermann, Hans H., *Weimar—Bestandsaufnahme einer Republik*, Reinbek bei Hamburg, 1969.

Hillgruber, Andreas, *Deutschlands Rolle in der Vorgeschichte der beiden Weltkriege*, Göttingen, 1967.

Katorowicz, Hermann, *Gutachten zur Kriegsschuldfrage 1914*, Frankfurt am Main, 1967.

Kolb, Eberhard, *Die Arbeiterräte in der deutschen Innenpoltik 1918–19*, Düsseldorf, 1962.

Kolb, Eberhard and Rürup, Reinhard, *Der Zentralrat der deutschen sozialistischen Republik*, Leiden, 1968.

Kucznski, Jürgen, *Studien zur Geschichte des deutschen Imperialismus*, Berlin, 1948–1950, 1 and 2.

Lindau, Rudolf, *Revolutionäre Kampfe, 1918–1919*, Berlin, 1960.

Matthias, E., *Zwischen Räten und Geheimräten: Die deutsche Revolutionsregierung 1918–1919*, Bonn, 1970.

Michaelis, Herbert and Schraepler, Ernst (eds.), *Ursachen und Folgen vom deutschen Zusammenbruch 1918 und 1945 bis zur staatlichen Neuordnung Deutschlands in der Gegenwart*, Berlin, 1958.

Mitchell, Allan, *Revolution in Bavaria 1918/1919*, Princeton, 1965.

Nelson, Keith, "The 'Black Horror on the Rhine'; Race as a Factor in Post-WW I Diplomacy," *Journal of Modern History*, vol. 42, no. 42, December 1970, pp. 606–28.

Nicholls, A. J., *Weimar and The Rise of Hitler*, New York, 1968.

Rosenberg, Arthur, *Die Enstehung der deutschen Republik*, Berlin, 1930, 2nd ed.

Ryder, A. J., *The German Revolution of 1918*, Cambridge, 1967.

Schmolze, Gerhard (ed.), *Revolution and Räterepublik in München*, Düsseldorf, 1969.

Taylor, A. J. P., *From Sarajevo to Potsdam*, London, 1966.

Thieme, Karl, *Judenfeindschaft: Darstellungen und Analysen*, Frankfurt am Main, and Hamburg, 1963.

Waldman, Eric, *The Spartacist Uprising of 1919*, Milwaukee, 1958.

Weber, Hermann, *Die Wandlung des deutschen Kommunismus*, Frankfurt am Main, 1969.

Wheeler-Bennet, J.W., *The Forgotten Peace*, New York, 1939.

Winzer, Otto, *Revolutionäre Traditionen des Kampfes der deutschen Arbeiterbewegung gegen Militarismus und Krieg*, Berlin, 1956.

[183]

Zechlin, Egmont, *Die deutsche Politik und die Juden im ersten Weltkrieg*, Göttingen, 1969.

Zinoviev, G., *Probleme der deutschen Revolution*, Hamburg, 1923.

Other Works

Abell, Walter, *The Collective Dream in Art*, New York, 1966.

Escarpit, Robert, *Sociologie de la littérature*, Paris, 1968.

Guilleminault, Gilbert, *Les Années folles, 1918–1927*, Paris, 1958.

Landes, David S., *The Unbound Prometheus*, Cambridge, 1969.

Lang, André, *Déplacements et villégiatures littéraires*, Paris, no date.

Lefebvre, Henri, *La Vie quotidienne dans le monde moderne*, Paris, 1968.

Index